JIHAD IS NOT TERRORISM

Title:	Jihad is Not Terrorism
English Rendering:	Shahid Chaudhry
Original Title:	Jihad*:* In Urdu
Author:	Ghulam Ahmad Parwez
Editor:	Khalid M. Sayyed
Typesetter:	Saleena Karim
Cover Art:	Rehan Khan
Publisher:	Islamic Dawn Society
	76 Park Road
	Ilford, Essex IG1 1SF
	Email: bazm.london@talktalk.net
1st Edition:	January 2008

ISBN 978-1-8479955-5-1

A Record of this Publication is available from the British Library

Jihad is Not Terrorism

Translated by Shahid Chaudhry

ISLAMIC DAWN SOCIETY

CONTENTS

GLOSSARY

Allah: Arabic/Quranic reference to the One God Who is the Lord God, the Creator and Sustainer of the entire universe and everything that is in it. *Allah* is not an exclusive name for a tribal deity of Muslims as some Christians, Jews and other non-Muslims erroneously believe. It is wrong to consider *Allah* as a name for God as God has no name, only Attributes.

Deen: (or *Din*) A term with no exact English equivalent, a 'Way of Life', and in the Islamic context, a social, political system based on Quranic Values. Deen is generally translated incorrectly in English as religion.

Eiman: According to the Holy Quran, the conviction that results from full mental acceptance and intellectual satisfaction. This kind of conviction gives one a feeling of *amn* – peace, inner contentment. In addition, a *Momin* is one who accepts the truth and acts in such a way that it ensures his own peace and helps him to safeguard the security of the rest of mankind. *Amn*, *Eiman* and *Momin* have a common root.

Momin: One who accepts the truth in such a way that it ensures his own peace and helps to safeguard the peace and security of the rest of mankind. *Alm'omin* is one of the Attributes of Allah Himself. See also *Eiman.*

Muhammad: (PBUH), the final Messenger of Allah.

PBUH: When Muslims take the name of a Messenger in writing, they usually add the salutation PBUH (Peace Be Upon Him). This salutation is not used in the Quran. It should be implicitly understood that, as mentioned in Surah *As-Saaffaat* (37:181), we do convey Peace upon all the Messengers of Allah, and Praise be to Allah, Sustainer of the Universe.

Quran: Holy Scripture of Muslims revealed by God Almighty to Prophet Muhammad (PBUH). Its literal meaning is collection, recitation. The Holy Quran is the last of the Divine books.

Rahmat: An Attribute of Allah by which He provides means of protection and sources of nourishment at every level, from the physical (nature, e.g. crops) to the psychological (for benefit of human self-development, e.g. Revelation (*Wahi*)).

Shariyat: Islamic Law, Way of Life. *Shariyat* is synonymous with *Deen.*

Note: With reference to Quranic verses cited in this book: The Surah number is written first followed by the verse number. For example, (4:6) means Surah No 4, Verse 6.

INTRODUCTION

Jihad – What the Quran states

Khalid Mahmood Sayyed

The shocking events of September 11, 2001 in the United States of America rocked the entire West as never before and changed the world for ever.. It has been the topic of the day ever since, dominating media reporting all over the globe. The USA, Britain and their allies formed a global coalition and bombed heavily the suspected strongholds of Osama bin Laden in Kandhar, Kabul and other parts of Afghanistan. Osama has never been found – dead or alive – but the Coalition's occupation of Afghanistan continues. The radical government of Iran is widely seen in the West as the sustaining force behind the power of militant organizations such as Hamas in the Middle East. The suicide bombing missions and terrorist activities in central London and the Madrid city-centre have made an intense situation even more so. The subsequent invasion of Iraq, with its never-ending carnage, has added fuel to the fire of distrust and animosity between the Christian West and the Muslim East. We are living the Crusades all over again: a vast number of people in the West equate such terrorist activities with Islam and consider most young Muslim men as potential terrorists and a threat to society while an ever-increasing number of Muslims, especially the young, are vigorously reviving in their hearts – and becoming more vocal about – the traditional Islamic sentiment of loathing towards non-Muslims, especially the Judeo-Christian world.

This is the burning issue, figuratively as well as literally, of the day and warrants our attention. It is important because the West – as well as a growing number of Muslims – believe activities such as suicide bombing and terrorist missions are not only sanctioned but actually encouraged by Islamic teachings; the term *jihad* is taken to mean 'armed combat against non-Muslims.'

Let us look at this issue intelligently, coolly and level-headedly from the standpoint of Islam.

Islam and the Quran

But, what is Islam? The question has been asked thousands of times and appears to be ridiculously simple. In reality, however, it is not as easy to answer as many might like to think. As has been realistically observed by some, one might distinguish *three* Islams: First, the Islam contained in the Quran; second, the Islam as interpreted and developed by theologians through the Prophetic Tradition (*Hadith*); it includes what is known as the *Sharia* as well as *fiqh* [the Islamic jurisprudence (law)] for legal purposes, and third, the Islam reflected in the deeds and achievements of Muslims through history as well as the present day. However, this may be too fine a distinction. What Muslims have done and achieved throughout their history, and still do, has largely been on the basis of the second Islam in the above list. At least, they have tried, and still do, to find a justification for most of their actions in Traditional Islam–the conventional view of Islam based upon an amalgam of *Hadith* (records of the sayings and deeds of Prophet Mohammad (PBUH)), *Taareekh* [historical records like *kutub al-maghaazi* (annals of raids and battles), *Sira tur Rasool* (biographical records of the Prophet)], *Tafseer* (the Quranic exegeses), as well as *Fiqh* (treatises on Jurisprudence).

Practically, that means that there is the Scripture (the Quran) and there is the interpretation of it (the extra-Quranic literature). At times, the two sources are at odds with one another and present different – sometimes, contradictory – views about a given subject. The result has been scores of brands and definitions of Islam solidifying those different views over more than fifteen centuries into as many sects of Islam. The logic commonly accepted and adhered to by the dominant majority of Muslims is as follows:

1. The Quran, the Divine Message was revealed to Mohammad (PBUH).
2. He had the duty to transmit, as well as explain and interpret, the Message.
3. He fulfilled his prophetic duty to the full by honestly transmitting God's Word (the Quran) to the people of Hejaz (whose duty in turn it was to spread the Message to the rest of the world); also, he explained and interpreted the Divine Message by his deeds as well as utterances.
4. Mohammad's explanations and interpretations were recorded by very able compilers, under the title *Hadith*,

after extremely careful and hard work that is almost flawless.

5. No one can ever understand God's Message better than the Messenger himself, who was directly guided by God. Therefore, in a way, *Hadith* is God's own explanation and interpretation of His Word.

It follows logically that if one finds a discrepancy between the Quran and *Hadith*,

1. the problem lies with the reader's understanding, and
2. the *Hadith* view overrides the Quranic view (because the reader's concept of the Quranic view is a misunderstanding in the first place and therefore faulty.

The problem is compounded by another term often used by Muslims – the *Sunna* (the Prophetic Model). Short for *Sunna tar Rasool Allah* (the way of the Messenger of Allah) or *Sunna tan Nabi* (the way of the Prophet), it is almost invariably used in conjunction with the term *Quran*. Muslims assert that Islamic laws must be based upon 'the Quran and the *Sunna*.' But, there we come up against a problem. In response to the question 'What / where is the Quran?' one can point out to a particular volume in a pile of books and say, 'Here is a volume in the Arabic language, consisting of 114 chapters, revealed to the Prophet Mohammad (PBUH) in 6th/7th century Arabia.' No one is likely to dispute that statement. But, the answer to the question 'What / where is the *Sunna*?' is not that easy to provide. The response is very likely to be: 'Well, the *Sunna* is contained in the various authentic compilations of *Hadith*, reliable records of *Taareekh* and *Sira*, and of course, the Quran.' So, the *Sunna* has to be compiled from all these sources. There have been scores of such compilations in various languages throughout the history of literature on Islam. The diversity of these sources has meant the appearance of differing versions of the Prophetic Model simply because of the inconsistencies of the source material. The result has been a very conspicuous absence of one authentic compilation of the *Sunna* unanimously agreed upon by Muslims. A more unfortunate consequence has been the division of the *umma* (the Muslim nation) into literally scores of sects believing in versions of Islamic philosophy and conduct based upon the Prophetic Model vastly different from - at times, opposite to – each other.

Confusion and contradiction

An impartial and critical examination of the extra-Quranic literature of Islam, such as *Hadith*, reveals differences not only between various reports on the same subject but also between *Hadith* and the Quran. Here are a couple of examples:

1. *Mut'a* (temporary marriage) is forbidden according to some reports while according to others it is permissible.

The Quran, however, does not sanction it; the Quranic marriage is intended for life in a loving and caring environment for both partners (30:21)

2. According to *Hadith*, the punishment for fornication is 100 lashes for the single (unmarried) and stoning to death for the married.

The Quran makes no such distinction and prescribes 100 lashes regardless:

> The woman and the man guilty of fornication, flog each of them with a hundred stripes; … (24:2)

In my view, therefore, the way forward for Muslims – if they desire to remove all that confusion that exists about what Islam teaches, may be the following:

According to the Quran, the canon is the Book of God, which was given to Mohammad (PBUH). His duty was to teach it to the people of his time in a manner which would make them understand it comprehensively so that they could pass it on to the rest of humanity for all times. This included their moral as well academic training, interpretation of the Message, and implementing it under the circumstances of the time. The collection of his actions and sayings is a valuable historical record which should serve as a precedent. It should be used to take guidance from as we do in taking lessons from history. They should help us to know how Mohammad (PBUH) and the people of his time viewed the fundamental principles of the Quran. The details in *Hadith* were never meant to become etched in stone for all eternity. Of all Muslim literature, only the Quran lays a serious claim to divinity, universality and eternity and as such, in the Muslim context, it should be the ultimate authority in matters of Faith. Also because only the Quran – and no other genre of Islamic literature - has been, and still is, to countless human beings the final, unadulterated, direct Word of the Creator. Thus, it is imperative that we look at the question of terrorism and *jihad* from the point of view of the Quran, the Muslim holy book.

Terrorism, or jihad? The Quranic perspective

As it has been so aptly remarked, more than half of the issues in a discussion are automatically addressed if the terminology involved is agreed upon before hand. Let us, therefore, determine what we mean by *terrorism*. Linguistically, 'terror' is described as: '1) intense, overwhelming fear; 2) Something, as a terrifying object or event that instils intense fear; 3) Ability to instil intense fear; 4) Violence promoted by a group to achieve or maintain supremacy. Also, (informal): One that is annoying or difficult to manage, especially a child ('nuisance'). [1]

This may be expressed in Arabic by the word *khawf*. Lexically, the word *khawf* springs from the three-letter root *kha, waao, fa,* which basically means 'to apprehend an imminent danger'.

In the Quran it is mentioned in Chapter 4, *An-Nisaa* (The Women):

> If a woman fears transgression from her (quarrelling) husband ... (4:128).

In Chapter 16, *An-Nahl* (The Bees), it states:

> They fear their Sustainer's supremacy and do as they are told … (16:50).

Therefore, 'fear of Allah' means to follow the right (Allah's) path for fear of the ill effects which will result by abandoning it. As we can see, *khawf* is just like the apprehension one has if one is to touch a naked flame. That is why *al-khafa* is the protective overall of bee-keepers.

Incidentally, *khawf* has also been used in the Quran in the applied meanings of armed combat (33:19). It also means 'to reduce' or decrease' (16:47).

Fear, therefore, is a negative feeling which can be avoided by following God's way as laid down in the Quran (2:38; 6:48, etc).

---

[1] Webster's E. E. New Riverside Dictionary (1984).

It can be deduced, therefore, that fear (terror) is not desirable and is to be avoided and averted. It just cannot be right for anyone to live in terror. Thus, the tactics used by any single person, or a group, or a state to try to achieve or maintain supremacy by instilling intense fear is wrong.

Secondly, one of the fundamentals of the Quranic teachings is that one cannot adopt negative (wrong) means to achieve an aim, even if it is positive (right). In other words, the end does NOT justify the means. The Quran states:

> We have shown him (Man) the (right) way–to take it or leave it. (76:3)

It also declares:

> The right path leads Man to the right end, the wrong to the wrong ... (4:88; 4:137; 4:143; 25:9)

Therefore, according to the Quran, instilling fear just cannot be accepted as legitimate – even if it is for the noble and exalted purpose of upholding Islam (God's law).

Thirdly, the terror tactics aimed at people who are not directly involved in, or responsible for, the conflict can NEVER be justified from the Quranic viewpoint. It states very clearly:

> No one shall bear someone else's burden. (6:165)

So, punishing innocent people for the misdeeds of men in power is totally un-Quranic.

Furthermore, such unjustifiable and misplaced killings are seen by the Quran as gigantic acts of murder:

> A single unjustified killing is tantamount to annihilating the entire human race ... (5:32; 6:152;17:33)

By the same token, bombing the helpless and innocent civilians in the poverty-stricken villages and towns of Afghanistan, or the peaceful multitudes in Iraqi cities, for the crimes of one person and his group cannot be justified from a Quranic perspective.

Fourthly, the Quran has laid down rules of conduct in times of both war and peace. Generally, one *must* be fair to everyone at *all* times:

> Be just and fair, even to your enemies. (5:8)

Elsewhere, it states:

> If you fear violation of an agreement by a nation, throw it away on the basis of equality ... (8:58)

Again, it reminds Muslims:

> In confrontation, remember a lot more, and adhere more strongly to, the Law of God – so that you come out benefited. (8:58)

Clearly, then, Muslims must conduct themselves fairly, honestly and openly, even in times of war. So, how can killing of innocent people, taking the hostages, etc. in times of peace be justified from an 'Islamic' viewpoint?

Jihad

What is *jihad* according to the Quran?

Linguistically, the term springs from the three-letter root *JhD* with the basic meanings of 'hardship', 'toiling' and 'completing a task' [according to *Taaj al Uroos,* the famous Arabic lexicon by Mohibuddin Al-Hanafi (d. 1791), published in Egypt, circa 1890). *Juhud* means 'expanse and energy'; but it may be used in the sense of 'toil' as in the Quranic verse 9:79. *Jahaad* means an arid grassless piece of land; *ajhadat lak al ard* means 'the land became visible / exposed for you.' Thus, the very well-known Islamic term for exercising judgment in matters of religious matters – *ijtehaad* - literally means 'to strive and exert fully.'

In the Quran we find the term *mujaahedeen* used as contrasting antonym for *q'aaedeen* (those who sit, not move); therefore, *mujaahedeen* means 'those who strive.'

Therefore, *jihad* is a comprehensive term for 'hard work, perseverance, striving' in the way of God. In the course of this striving, one may face extreme hardship which may sometimes culminate in armed combat (but only for defence). For 'armed combat', the Quranic term is *qitaal* (killing) *fi sableel Allah* (in the way of God). So, *jihad* in the meaning of 'armed combat' is a misnomer – it should be *qitaal;* and *jihad* in the sense of terrorism has no place whatsoever in the Quranic perspective.

These are some of the points which Ghulam Ahmad Parwez has very ably tackled in his article. Parwez (1903-1985) founded the *Tolu-e-Islam* (Dawn of Islam) movement in 1938 in British India and launched its mouthpiece Urdu journal, the monthly *Tolu-e-Islam* which continues to be published from Lahore, Pakistan. The movement stands for a rational interpretation of the Quran which it considers as the final authority on all matters Islamic, superseding any extra-Quranic literature.

It is hoped that this introduction and the following article will remove most, if not all, confusion, misunderstanding and apprehension surrounding the very crucial current subject of terrorism and *jihad*, putting these concepts in their true Quranic light.

Khalid Sayyed
Peterborough, UK.

JIHAD

Ghulam Ahmad Parwez

Disclaimer

The following work is a translation and as such any ambiguity in the text is the responsibility of the translator and not the original author.

1
PROPAGANDA

Propaganda is an art perfected throughout the ages by people like Goebbels, the propaganda secretary of Hitler. Goebbelian truth, as we all know it to be, is based on the principle that a lie uttered a hundred times becomes gospel truth. How much this theory has been successful in varying fields is hard to measure, but it has certainly played a vital role in maligning Islam. A gloss over the pages of history furnishes ample evidence as to how Islam and its message have been distorted by propaganda.

Europe's Revenge

During the course of her history Europe were united on one platform only once. And, unfortunately for the human world, this unity led to barbarous Crusades against Islam. Defeat in these wars was a soul-racking and heart-burning shock for Europe. With the passage of time these hurt feelings have somewhat been assuaged. But there is still a deep scar in her subconscious. This splinter has always troubled her, and she has always fretted and fumed to avenge this defeat.

There are mainly two ways of taking revenge. One is to tread the path of Genghis and Halegu and thereby spill blood on the pages of history. But this style from the Dark Ages is considered out of fashion these days. During the days of Genghis, man had not as yet learnt the art of diplomacy. He did not know to sugar-coat his malicious intentions. He did not know to hide his sharpened nails in soft paws. He did not know how to cover his acts of tyranny and oppression with the silken veil of welfare and development. Whatever he did, he did openly, declared his intentions and then acted. But man has changed. He has progressed in 'intellect and wisdom', and in 'knowledge and vision'. As such, today, an open mitigation of his lust for blood would amount to stupidity. Now the most successful person is he who exploits others without letting them know that they have been taken for a ride. He snatches the essential resources of life in such a subtle manner that nobody suspects him to be a robber. In the guise of mentor and reformer he may destroy an entire community while the victims remain unaware as to what is happening to them.

Oppression and destruction committed by the people of the Age of Ignorance was like a whirlwind that comes with grating roar, tremulous cadence, and whose uproar and tumult even the blind can see and the deaf can hear. But the moves of a deceitful person, in the present age of intellect and reason, are like a calm river in which there is neither uproar nor agitation of waves; it is a river that remains as silent as a Church with neither commotion nor buffeting of waves. But deep under its surface lurk dragons and alligators ready to pounce upon and engulf entire communities, while eyes do not see them and ears do not hear them.

This serene and subtle method of obliteration and squandering is – propaganda.

Propaganda is an invisible fire. It quietly reduces all conviction and sagacity to ashes with no smoke so as to warn of the imminent danger. Propaganda is a silent and organised conspiracy which slowly but gradually, without noise or tumult, changes the nature and character of things in such a manner that one without realizing loses one's capacity to differentiate between beneficial and harmful, between good and bad, and between virtuous and evil. As a result, the conspirators become so powerful that they can make one accept what they like and that too in the manner they like. Thus propaganda becomes a trick of such manipulators as Samiri, the Biblical character, who successfully persuaded Israelites to revert to idol (calf) worship in the absence of Moses. Owing to this, individuals as well as nations become worse than cattle. The Quran states:

> They have hearts wherewith they understand not, they have eyes wherewith they see not, they have ears wherewith they hear not (i.e. despite having their own faculties of thinking, seeing and hearing they look up to others for guidance) as such they are not human beings. They are as the cattle, nay, but they are worse. (7:179)

The Picture of Islam

Capitalist Europe used this trick of Samiri in order to avenge her defeat at the hands of Islam. She used the propaganda weapon in such an organised but quiet manner that Islam appeared to the world what it definitely is not. With the help of the pen and a rumour-mongering campaign so dreadful a picture of Islam has been drawn that even Muslims themselves will shiver to the core if they happen to see it. Consequently, today, wherever in the civilised and cultured world Islam is mentioned, bloodstained scenes of murder and plunder, death and destruction, oppression and tyranny, injustice and despotism appear one by one as if one is watching a motion picture.

Gangs of savage and bloodthirsty wild folks, spears and swords in hand, are coming from all sides like floods of misfortune. Who are these barbarous people? Are they jinn, horrible demons or giants? Amidst slogans of 'Allahu Akbar' they are spitting venom and shedding blood. Is this Divine wrath? This rage of fury is destroying culture and civilisation, fairness and justice, continence and chastity, religion and faith. Besides, one by one they are uprooting flowers, fruits and shadowy trees. Whatever knowledge and talent thousands of years of human effort and inquiry has earned is being wiped off like chaff and rubbish. Prayers of the oppressed, crying and weeping of orphans, lamentations and plaints of widows are not eliciting a Divine response. O God of this dreadful Community! Art Thou doors closed for the poor of this world? This unusual calamity is turning human habitations into deserts, settlements into ruins, libraries into ashes, lofty buildings and palaces, the symbols of culture and civilisation, into ruins. Heaps of broken Crosses, truckloads of sacred beads, deserted temples and demolished Churches can be seen everywhere. No one is at peace or safe; neither a Brahmin nor a Christian monk, neither women nor children. Some have been killed, others have been taken captive and are being whipped by barbarous Sheikhs so as to force them to the slave market and thereby sell respectable human beings for a princely sum.

Ideology of Peace and Security

Such is the picture of Islam that has been drawn with the weapon of propaganda. And these self-styled painters of hate have deliberately ignored the fact that the fundamental teaching of Islam leads man to the path of peace.

> O people of the book there has come to you from Allah The Light (of Truth) and a perspicuous Book which is unambiguous in its teachings and through this Book Allah will open ways of peace and security for those who lead their lives in accordance with the Divine laws. (5:15-16)

The Book of Allah leads humanity to the door of peace and safety.

> For them (who took the straight path ordained by Allah) is an abode of peace with their Sustainer, and He is their Protecting Friend because of what good acts they do. (6:128)

It is the same abode of peace and security to which Allah invites them.

> And Allah calls to an abode where everything is safe and protected. And whoever desires (success), Allah guides him to the straight path. (10:25)

In that abode the objective of all ideas and deeds and endeavour and inquiry is a paradise of safety.

> And doubtlessly, people who lead their lives according to the Divine laws will enjoy the bliss of gardens and water springs. (And it would be said to them), 'Enter these gardens in Peace and Security.' (15:45-46).

Against Disorder

One of the attributes of Allah, Who revealed Islam, is *Al-Momin*, which means 'One Who guarantees universal peace'. Another attribute of Allah is *As-Salam*, which means 'peace'. In fact, the word Islam itself means peace. And its followers are called *Momin*, i.e. people responsible for establishing peace. Thus a Muslim is one who follows in totality the eternal laws of Allah as enshrined in the Holy Quran so as to establish peace and prosperity not only for himself but also for the whole of humankind.

We have seen that the fundamental message of Islam is peace and security. Therefore, it declares that those who indulge in corruption, disorder and breaches of peace deserve Divine wrath. In this context see *Surah Ar-Ra'd* where it states that those who fulfill their pledge to Allah and do not breach their covenant, for them is the recompense of a final, happy abode and they would be extended salutations of peace and security. On the other hand, for those who break the covenant with Allah and create disorder and mischief in the land, is the terrible home:

> (Without doubt) for them awaits gardens of perpetual bliss. They shall enter there along with the righteous, among their fathers, their spouses and their offspring and *mala'ika* (Forces of Nature) shall enter unto them from every gate (with the salutation), "Peace unto you for whatever trials you have endured with steadfastness." Now how excellent is the final home of these people. But those who break the covenant of Allah after ratifying it, and cut asunder those things which Allah has commanded to be joined, and create disorder and mischief in the land; for them is the terrible home. (13:23-25)

The Quran mentions in explicit terms that a faith that spreads evil and destruction on earth is unacceptable to Allah.

> When these people gain power then their entire effort is to spread chaos and mischief in the land. They destroy crops, cattle and human beings, but Allah does not like what they do. (2:205)

The religion of such people is *fisq* and they are *fasiqin*. Thus they are diametrically opposed to *momin*.

According to the laws of Allah *fasiqin* are on the wrong path.

> (Who is a *fasiq*? A person who breaks the covenant of Allah after ratifying it is a *fasiq*; a person who severs human relationships by fragmenting humanity into pieces on the basis of unnatural racial or national distinctions is a *fasiq*; a person who creates disorder and mischief in the land is a *fasiq*.) They do not live within the limits prescribed by the Divine laws. They cut asunder what Allah has ordered to be joined. (With their evil deeds and waywardness) they create chaos and mischief in the land. Indeed they are in the loss. (2:26-27)

The Quran forbids man in unambiguous terms to follow the path of perdition and destruction and openly states:

> And (listen) after reforming and setting the country in order, do not create disorder and mischief. If you are fearful of losing something or have a desire to gain something, in both the situations, act according to Allah's laws. Allah's *Rahmat* (means of protection and sources of nourishment) is close to those who lead a balanced life in accordance with His laws. (7:56)

Janna is an abode where one can live in peace and security. As such, the doors of this eternal home are not open to those who adopt the path of waywardness and transgression and thereby create chaos and disorder on earth. The Quran, without mincing words, states:

> As for the Abode of the Hereafter We assign it unto those who intend not high-handedness, seek not oppression or corruption and mischief on earth. The sequel is for those who ward off (evil and establish peace on earth as per Divine laws). (28:83)

The Quran narrates stories of nations dead and communities gone by. Why? The answer is simple: we must learn from history that creating disorder and mischief on earth is a crime against humanity and it results in destruction and obliteration. The biggest charge that the Quran levels against the Pharaoh and his people is that they were evildoers for they divided people into sections and instigated one section to oppress the other. (28:4 and 28:14)

The Pharaoh was an emblem of tyranny and oppression. His compatriot *Qarun* (Korah of the Bible) was an embodiment of capitalism. Along with politics of tyranny, capitalism creates disorder and chaos on earth. Therefore, the Quran states that *Qarun* was also a *mufsid* (evildoer) (28:76-77). After narrating the conditions and affairs of the nations dead, the Quran asks with regret as to why there have not been people in those nations to prevent men from creating chaos and disorder in the earth (11:116).

The Quran consistently repeats the tales of the rise and fall of the Children of Israel so that one may draw lessons from their crimes:

> As often as they light a fire for war, Allah extinguishes it (through other people). Their effort is for spreading disorder in the land and Allah does not like such *mufsideen* (designers of chaos). (5:64)

The Advent of the last Messenger

Indeed the objective of the advent of the last Messenger of God, Muhammad, with the message of Islam, was to establish an order on earth in accordance with the Divine laws because, at that point of time in history, there was complete waywardness, disorder and chaos in thought and action of all the societies of the world. The Quran states:

> (We have sent the Messenger of Islam because owing to the misdeeds of the people) disorder and corruption has engulfed both land and sea. As such, We want that Our (Law of Requital) should make them taste a part of that which they have earned. It is possible that people (after seeing the destructive results of their misdeeds may repent) and return (to the straight path of Allah). (30:41)

It is for this reason that the first point in the call of the last Messenger refers to prohibiting disorder and chaos in the land of Allah.

When they are asked not to spread disorder in society, they retort audaciously: "We do not spread disorder. We are those who promote order and peace." Of a surety, they are the ones who spread disorder but they realise it not (because they do not have a true perception of right and wrong). (2:11-12)

Consequently the Quran regards disorder as the opposite of conviction and good deeds. The two cannot co-exist:

> Shall Our Law of Requital treat those who have *eiman* (believing in the Divine Guidance with reason and knowledge) and work deeds of righteousness, the same as those who spread disorder and corruption on earth? Shall Our law of Requital treat those who obey and follow the laws of Allah the same as those who turn away from the Divine path? (Remember this is against Our law of Requital). (38:28)

Reconciliation and Peace

These then are the basic principles of Islam. Now should the picture drawn by the propagandists of this system of life be considered a true one? Did this system guarantee peace and security in the world or did it promote disorder and corruption in the world? The answers to these questions are surely in the negative. It has been unfortunate for the human world that the message of peace and reconciliation was considered to be oppressive and tyrannical. The antidote was taken as poison. The sick humanity shunned it believing that her illness was incurable and consequently met a miserable doom.

In fact, according to the teachings of the Quran, a Muslim is not allowed to use violence unjustly. And the height of tolerance is that if a non-Muslim abuses him, he cannot respond likewise. For instance, if a follower of another religion uses derogatory words against the respected

Last Messenger, a Muslim must not pay back in the same coin. The reason: the Quran states that to every nation was sent a Messenger and a Muslim has to believe in all of them whether their names and details are mentioned in the last revealed Book or not. Therefore, a Muslim has to be cautious; chances are that the founder of the religion to which that non-Muslim belongs might be a genuine, respected messenger of Allah. Leaving religious figures of non-Muslims aside, the Quran goes to the extent:

> The deities whom these people associate with Allah are no doubt false. This does not mean, however, that you may revile them. You should not revile them lest ignorance in these people revile Allah in retaliation. They adhere to their beliefs because they seem fair to them. The nature of their deeds will become clear to them on the Day of Reckoning. (6:109)

Equity and Justice

Not only are the feelings of others to be respected but also they are to be dealt with in equity and justice. In fact there is unparalleled emphasis on equity and justice in the Quran. It repeatedly asks to judge justly.

> (O Muslims) Allah orders you that you restore deposits to there owners, and, if you judge between people, that you judge justly. (4:58)

> And again:

> (O Muslims) Allah orders you to do justice to all (in all matters) and (apart from this) make good the deficiencies of others. (16:90)

Truthful Testimony

Justice is based on evidence and testimony. In this context the teaching of the Quran is:

> (O Muslims) if you are called upon to testify, do not appear as a witness on behalf of either party, but for Allah. Be truthful in testifying even though it may be against your own-selves or your parents and kinfolks, whether the party concerned is rich or poor.

Allah safeguards the interests of both the parties. Do not follow your own inclinations lest you should swerve from justice. Do not foist your statements nor show aversion to appearing as a witness. Allah is well aware of what you do. (4:135)

Aiding a Culprit the Greatest Offence

According to the Quran the greatest offence is to help a culprit. In context of the story of Hazrat Musa (Moses) it is stated:

> (Musa said), "O my Sustainer! For as much as you have favoured me, I will never more be supporter of the guilty." (28:17)

Justice to Enemy

With regards to justice the Quran establishes a very sublime concept. To deal justly with friends is a common human conduct. To be just to strangers is also understandable. But, take a community who is in open enmity with you and is always working to harm you. It does not leave any stone unturned to destroy you. Now this community, or one of its members, comes to you seeking justice. What will you do if the evidence in the case points against your own community or its members? Will you be just? If you are a Muslim, you have to be just in such a situation also. This is called *min-azmil umuuri*. The Quran states:

> O Muslims! Always stand up for justice in the cause of Allah. Let not the enmity of others towards you deviate you from the path of justice. Always and in all circumstances act justly. This is akin to *taqwa* (obeying and following the Divine laws). Remember Allah is aware of all that you do. (5:8)

The maxim 'Love thy enemy' is mere romantic poetry. It is impossible for a person to love his enemy; it runs against human nature. But justice to the enemy is possible. And all those who are aware of the Divine laws know that in order to turn this possibility into a reality you need large-heartedness, magnanimity, courage, strength and sublime character. The Quran helps you to develop these qualities. 'Deal justly with your enemy' is a teaching that is hard to find in any code of law apart from the Quran. Despite these teachings of Islam it is portrayed as a religion of oppression and tyranny. Is it fair and just to do so? No. It is a deliberate act of ignoring truth and justice.

Unjust Killing

The Quran has introduced the world to the inspiring principle of Oneness of God and respect of humanity. This shows that in Islam human life is if immense value. And to kill a person is a grave offence under its constitution. In order to elaborate upon the honour and value it attaches to human life the Quran has adopted a very eloquent and comprehensive style. On one hand, it gives a universal principle of Oneness of God, and on the other, it snubs and reprimands unjust killings of human beings.

Unjust murder is such a heinous crime that Allah ordained for the Children of Israel that if anyone slew a person, unless it be as a punishment for murder or for spreading disorder in the land, it would be as if he slew the whole mankind. On the other hand if anyone saved a life it would be as if he saved the life of the whole mankind. (5:32)

Blood Money

It is possible that, despite all these prohibitions, one might accidentally kill a person. To deal with such a situation the Quran lays down a life-saving and just principle called *Qisas*, i.e. punishment proportionate to the crime. Murder may be with or without intent. In the case of the former the punishment is death (no blood-money) or, depending upon the nature of the crime, a punishment less severe than the maximum penalty (4:93). In other words, the punishment should be commensurate with the crime (42:40; 17:33). If the heirs of a victim voluntarily, or out of goodwill, wish to forego the blood money, or a part thereof, they have the right to do so (17:33). In such a situation it is necessary that the culprit carry out the terms of the agreement faithfully and with good grace. If he violates the agreement he should be punished severely.

Robbery and Looting

For looting, robbery, plunder, destruction and other related crimes the Quran has laid down specific punishments for the offender, whether he is a Muslim or a non-Muslim.

Islam and the Sword

The ignorant and biased world has levelled one major charge against Islam that it owes its spread to the sword because people were forcibly converted to it. This charge clearly shows that when a person is blinded by the rage to take revenge and the passion to oppose, he ignores even hard obvious facts. He refuses to see explicit teachings that need no commentary or exposition. The Quran is not an ambiguous book that only a few select can understand; it is not a book of secret knowledge; it is not meant to be kept concealed; it is not in any dead language that one cannot understand. It is in plain and simple Arabic and is globally available. It has been translated into almost every language of the world. If one wants to know the teachings of Islam, one just has to buy a copy of the Quran and read it. But only a person in search of reality and desirous of the truth would make such an effort and not one whose motive is to defame Islam with malicious propaganda. Such will divert the attention of the people from the Quran (the basis of Islam) and entangle them in concocted history and misleading Traditions so as to make them agreeable. According to the Quran, *Eiman* (conviction based upon reason and knowledge) is related to the heart of a man. If heart and intellect do not accept something, it cannot be called *Eiman.* As such, *Eiman* and compulsion are contrary to each other. The Quran clearly states that if Allah had willed, He could have forced all men to move in a single direction like all other things of this universe. But this was not the Divine Plan. Man's right to free choice was not to be curbed.

> If Allah had willed He could have made you one community (i. e. He could have forced you all to move in one direction). But (as you see, He has not done so) so that He may let you develop by (right to free choice) which He has given to you. So vie one with another in good deeds. After all, you shall all return to Him and then He will inform you of (the truth and reality of) that wherein you differed. (5:48)

> At another location the Quran is more specific;

> If human beings had not been endowed with freedom of choice, all those who dwell on earth would have been forced to believe. But this was not Allah's way. His law is that man should be given an opportunity to exercise his right to free choice. Would you then, O Messenger! Compel them to believe in Islam? (10:99)

Similarly in *Surah Al-Anaam* it states:

> If Allah had willed all men would have followed a single path and none would have added anything in the Divine laws on his own. (But, as you see, He has endowed men with the right to free choice. Now you can only show them the right path, you cannot force them onto it). This is why We have not appointed you a guardian over them or responsible for their conduct. (6:108)

Men's Right to Free Choice

The Quran states that Allah has explicitly revealed the truth; it is left to man to either accept or reject it.

> Say: (It is) the truth from your Sustainer. Then whosoever will, let him accept, and whosoever will, let him reject. (18:29)

For those who accept this truth, their Self will complete the evolutionary phases of life and thereby enable them to reach their destination. And those who reject it will be deprived of this felicity.

> Allah has revealed the truth clearly. Whoever reflects on it, will do so to his advantage. On the other hand, those who choose to remain blind to it will do so to their own disadvantage. Remember, the Messenger is not your keeper to force you to reflect. We have made the truth so clear in diverse ways that those who reflect on it, exclaim: "You have (O Messenger) indeed separated the grain from the chaff". In this way We have made it manifest to a people who are disposed to understand. (6:105-106)

This fact is more eloquently depicted elsewhere:

> Say: "O mankind! The Truth from your Sustainer has certainly come to you. One who comes to be guided by it will be guided to one's own advantage. But, one who chooses to go astray, will only harm oneself. I am in no way responsible to protect you from the consequences of your wrong doings (because I cannot force you onto the right path)." (10:108)

Allah has lighted this world with His revelation and given man the faculty of intellect to ponder over it. Now it is for man to accept the right path or, if he wants to meet his doom, he can choose the wrong path.

> Lo! We have shown him the way of the truth and it is for him to accept it or reject it. (76:3)

The Quran contains permanent values as revealed by Allah. Anyone can seek guidance from it.

> So whosoever may heed. (74:55)

The Quran cautions those who invite people to the path of Allah. It states that they should preach this message with reason, logic, wisdom and exhortation.

> O Messenger! Do not entangle yourself with them. You continue your program of inviting people to the way of Allah with wisdom and kindly exhortation and discuss matters with them in the best possible manner. Allah knows best who is following the right path and who has gone astray. (16:125)

Those responsible for extending an invitation to the way of Allah should appeal to the intellect, prudence, insight and discernment of people; only then they will be able to influence them by the principles of Islam.

> (O Messenger, tell them), "My way and that of my followers is very clear and straight. My call is based on firm conviction and reason. My followers also follow this (style of inviting to the way of Allah with reason and subtle preaching). Allah is much above our setting up peers to Him." (12:108)

Compulsion and Duress is Despotism

The Quran warns us by recounting particular details of fallen nations that wayward and despotic rulers abrogated men's right to freedom of expression and owing to their dominating power forced their religion on others. In context of Hazrat Shuaib (Jethro of the Bible) and his people it states:

> The leaders of the arrogant party among his people (who were intoxicated with power and wealth) said, "O Shuaib, we will certainly drive you and your followers out of our city, or you will have to accept our religion." He replied, "Are you going to force your religion on us even though we abhor it?" (7:88)

And at a number of places it is mentioned in the Quran that when the court priests ('magicians' of the Bible) of Pharaoh saw the truth and declared their convinced faith in the Sustainer (God) of Hazrat Musa (Moses), the arrogant Pharaoh exclaimed:

> (Pharaoh) said: "You believe (in Musa) without my permission? Surely, he is your chief. He has imparted to you spurious knowledge. Be sure now, I will cut off your hands and your feet alternately, and I shall crucify you on the trunks of palm trees, and you shall know for certain which one of us can inflict sterner and more lasting punishment." (20:71)

Acceptance under Duress is Invalid

The Messengers (Prophets of God) came to eradicate this tyranny, despotism, domination and injustice. As such, the objective of Islam is to wipe off despotism and compulsion so as to create an atmosphere in which man has the rights of freedom of expression and free choice. Now, consider a supposition: a man is steadfast in conviction but is compelled to violate the Divine laws; should he be considered a transgressor? In the light of the Quranic teachings the answer to this question is in the negative. Acceptance under duress does not amount to belief (16:106). So acceptance of *Kufr* (ideas opposed to the Quran) under compulsion does not make you a *Kafir* (Rejector), who rejects the teachings of Islam. Similarly, acceptance of Islam under coercion would not make one a Muslim. The Quran is very cautious in this regard. For instance, some Bedouins were impressed by the power and majesty of the Muslims and accepted Islam. The Quran said to them, "Do not call yourselves 'Believers'; you have merely submitted to the political system of Islam - *Eiman* (belief in the Divine Guidance with reason and knowledge) has not entered your hearts." (49:12). Therefore, to be a Muslim *Eiman* should reach the depths of your heart. This means that there should be no contradiction between your thoughts, utterances and actions; they should all be in accordance with the Divine Guidance as enshrined in the Quran. Can this type of *Eiman* be created under duress? Obviously, not.

Apostasy

Leaving non-Muslims aside, even if a Muslim develops doubts about the truth of Islam, will he remain a Muslim? The answer is again in the negative. The reason is obvious: a man is free to enter the fold of Islam and he is at liberty to leave it. Therefore, the Quran does not prescribe any punishment for apostasy. No one must be terrified by threats of punishment into staying within Islam, nor must one be forced to become a Muslim. The very idea is meaningless.

No Compulsion in Islam

Now let us come to the verse that is the final word in this regard. This verse is enough evidence to remove all doubts about the matter. The Quran states:

> [If Allah, the possessor of such might, had desired then His order could have been established in the human sphere as it is in the natural sphere, but He did not wish to exercise compulsion.] There is no compulsion in Islam. Through His revelation Allah has made the right and the wrong path clear and left men free to choose either path (18:29, 90:10, 76:3). Whoever turns away from the wrong path of oppressive forces and comes to the right one has grasped the trustworthiest handhold, which will never break. Allah is all Knowing and all Hearing. (2:256)

There is nothing more to say in this context because 'the right direction has been made distinct from the wrong one' (2:256).

Why, then, all the fighting?

There is no compulsion in Islam; Islam is an ideology of peace and guarantees security; Islam is all for reconciliation and peace. Why on earth, then, are the pages of the Quran, books of history and biographies of the last Messenger filled with episodes of war? In fact, biographies of the last Messenger penned by the earlier writers talk more about wars than the life, times and character of the son of Abdullah.

Doubts have arisen about war and related questions because Islam has classed as 'religion'. Islam is **not** a religion. In fact, it is a challenge to Religion because it is *Deen*. There is a subtle difference between religion and *Deen*. If one ignores this difference then all sorts of doubts and confusions crop up.

Religion and Deen

Religion involves a private and personal relationship between man and God. This relationship does not concern itself with man's worldly life for which he requires another system called the State or Government. In religion, God is just an object of worship. Man is the worshiper and God is the worshiped. But Islam is not religion. It is *Deen*. The word *mazhab* (religion) is not even mentioned in the Quran.

In comparison, *Deen* is the entire system of life. It encompasses each and every aspect of human life. When one ponders on the varying aspects of human life, one realises that the word *Deen* used by the Quran in this context is both eloquent and comprehensive.

In comparison to all other creations man is born without the means to defend himself. In order to protect and defend himself he is dependent on collective life or society. As such, man is defined as a social animal.

Society is dependent on rules, regulation and laws because when a man leads a social life the effect of his thoughts and actions are not confined to him alone. Therefore, it is not possible for a human society to survive without rules and laws.

The system under which this society survives is called 'the state' in modern terminology. This system is called 'System of State'. It has one central authority that maintains the social norms and rest of the members of this State remain obedient and subordinate to that authority.

The members of a State adopt this life of obedience and subservience because it is beneficial to them. As such a social system will have the following organs:

– Central authority
– Obedience and subservience of the members
– A constitution that is to be followed
– Effects of this on life
– System of State

The Quran introduces this system of state with a comprehensive term of *Deen*. Ever since man attained consciousness and started living in a society he has developed and adopted varying methods of establishing a State. During the ancient period man led a nomadic life where tribes were governed by autocratic chieftains. Times changed. Man graduated to dictatorship, to nationalism, to fascism, to communism, to democracy, and so on. Though these are all different types of States but they differ only in form and not in character. The underlying spirit governing these types of States in all ages has always been the same. These States were formed on the basis of race, language, colour and nation, and on the belief that some people have the right to draft laws for the rest of the people. But the Quran declared that these types of States and the basis of forming them are all fabricated by men and therefore in the wrong. Unity of ideology should be the basis for establishing a State, I.e. a group of people believing in one particular ideology of life are members of one community and citizens of one State. And the basis of such a State is that no man has the right to draft laws for other men; only Allah has the right to formulate immutable laws. As such, in this system only Allah is the Central Authority and sovereignty lies with Him alone. Since the natural outcome of belief in Oneness of the Creator is unity amongst the created, the foundation of this system is based on justice.

The Meaning of Justice

Justice under manmade laws means decisions in accordance with the law current at any given time. For instance, at one time consumption of alcohol was prohibited in America. Anyone found violating this law was punished and it was considered just. Now this law has been repealed and, consequently, alcohol consumers cannot be questioned or punished. Today this is considered justice. So manmade laws change with time and space. They are relative, not absolute. As such, it is possible that a decision that is considered 'just' may not be just at all. At the most one can say that the decision is in accordance with the laws in use.

The laws of Allah, as stated earlier, are immutable and based on the absolute truth. So, the decisions taken on their basis would be absolutely and really just. In this system justice would mean that every individual is provided with equal means and opportunities to develop their latent faculties. This way they will achieve their deserved status in society in accordance with their developed faculties. Therefore the salient features of the *Deen* that has been introduced by the Quran to the world are:

- In this State central authority and sovereignty lies only with Allah.
- All members of this community are equally obedient and subservient to the laws of Allah.
- The fundamental laws and principles of this State are enshrined and preserved in the Quran.
- The practical outcome of this system is justice which every member of the State is responsible for establishing. If (s)he fails to perform his/her duty (s)he will be held accountable in the Court of Allah.
- This then is *Ad-Deen*. It is also called Islam. Every Messenger, from the first to the last, propagated the same *Deen*.

Messengers (Prophets of God) came to establish this *Deen*. But once they were no more, their followers used to reduce it to 'religion'. For instance, during the time of Hazrat Isa (Jesus Christ) the Jews had totally abandoned the concept of *Deen*. That is why the Jews opposed Hazrat Isa who wanted them to revolt against the despotic rule of the Romans. But, to the Jews, it meant an end to their religious hegemony. So they started opposing the son of Mary.

The last Messenger, Muhammad, also came to establish this *Deen*. The Jews and the Christians had disfigured the original message of *Deen* to such an extent that when the last Messenger appeared, the Bible had already been filled with non-divine teachings like – 'render therefore to Caesar the things that are Caesar's, and to the Church the thing that are Church's.'(Luke 21/25). In other words, *Deen* (the affairs of the Hereafter) was had been separated from the affairs of the world (the Here). Oneness had given way to Duality. It happened because *Deen* was replaced by 'religion'. Religion was monasticism for the masses and governance was the right of Caesar. The Quran came to eradicate all these anomalies, so it declared:

> The monasticism which they invented for themselves was not prescribed by Allah for them. (57:27)

Allah sent only *Deen* through His Messengers. This *Deen* is:

> The only *Deen* prescribed by Allah for all humanity is Islam. This was given also to the earlier Messengers but their followers

created differences through mutual jealously. Allah's law of Requital is that whoever rejects the Divine guidance Allah is Swift in calling him to account. (3:19)

The Practical form

The basic characteristic and fundamental distinction from other systems of *Deen* is that in it requires one to obey the laws of Allah and no one else.

> (O Messenger) follow that what is revealed to you and wait steadfastly till Allah settles the issue between you and your opponents. He is the best of all judges. (10:109)

The Meaning of Ibada

This obedience and subservience is termed *ibada* in the Quran. (This comprehensive Quranic term is commonly – but erroneously – is translated into English as 'worship' and regrettably has been taken as such in the entire corpus of conventional Islam). *Ibada* literally means slavery and subservience. As such, the relationship of man and Allah is of that of Master and slave and not that of worshiper and the worshiped. Please recall the sermon of Hazrat Yusuf (the Biblical Joseph) - that provided him comfort in the dark cells of jail - which makes it very clear that authority and the right to rule rests only with Allah (*inil-Hukmu illaa lillaah*, 12:40): therefore, obey and be slave of Allah only (*amara allaa ta-buduuu illaaa iy-yaah*, 12:40). The two passages make the meaning of *ibada* very clear.

> (O Messenger) say to them: "I am but a human being like you with the only difference that it has been revealed to me that the entire authority rests with Allah the One; let him who believes in His law of Requital do that which is right, and not to obey anyone other than Allah and thus associate any authority with Him."
> (18:110)

A little earlier in the same chapter it states:

He allows none to share His governance. (18:26)

Therefore, according to the Quran, *ibada* is not 'worship' but is to become obedient and subservient to Allah. So, when a slave of Allah states *iyya-ka nabuuduu* ('we obey only You – 2:5) to Him with humility, he accepts being the obedient slave of Allah and in this way he is in fact sounding the bugle of revolution by *Deen* against 'religion'.

Religion and Politics

Manmade laws divide human life into two compartments of religion and politics. Accordingly, God becomes an object of worship whereas 'worldly' affairs are governed by manmade laws of the land. At the time of the advent of the last Messenger this duality was at its peak and consequently there was chaos and disorder in the entire world. Indeed the last Messenger came to eradicate this duality. Dr. Muhammad Iqbal [1] states:

> *Foundation of the Church upon monasticism was laid,*
> *How could kingship in mendicancy be contained?*
> *Royalty and monk-hood between them contended,*
> *It is exaltation, the other debasement;*
> *Politics freed itself from Faith,*
> *Nothing did holiness of the old man of the Church avail;*
> *When separation took place between wealth and religion,*
> *All that was left was over-lordship of desire,*
> *Duality is the misfortune of State and Religion,*
> *Duality is the benightedness of civilisation's eye,*
> *It is the miracle of a desert-dweller,*
> *Bearing of good tidings is synonymous with warning;*
> *Safety of mankind in it lies,*
> *That sufi* [the mystic] *and the King become one.* [2]

This was the thought that the last Messenger propagated among people who had broken their covenant with Allah (that subservience is only for Allah). These people were spreading chaos and disorder on earth

---

[1] Dr. Muhammad Iqbal (1877-1938) was the foremost Islamic philosopher of the last century as well as a poet and political leader. He is considered the spiritual father of Pakistan, having advocated a free Muslim state in India in 1930, though he never lived to see Pakistan appear on the map.

[2] M. Iqbal, *Baal-e-Jibril*

because they had violated the laws of Allah by dissociating politics from religion.

> (Who are *Fasiqin*? They are people) who break their covenant with Allah and who sunder what Allah has ordered to be joined. They, thus, create disorder and mischief in earth (with their misdeeds). (But little do they realise that by doing so) they cause loss (only) to themselves. (2:27)

Power and Authority

No system of State can be established without power. Law becomes law only when there is an authority to implement it. The Quran in the following inspiring words states this fact:

> (O people) this is a fact that We had sent aforetime Our Messengers with unambiguous proofs and sent with them the Book (of law) and balance (of right and wrong), that men may strive to establish justice. And We sent down (the sword of) iron in which is great might, as well as many benefits for mankind, that Allah may test who it is that will help (in establishing the *Deen* of) the Unseen and His Messengers: for Allah is full of strength and exalted in might. (57:25)

The State system is established by the Book (law) and iron. [3] Law without the power of implementation is nothing but a code of ethics. Religious leaders often preach this in their sermons the audiences enjoy sermons hoping that God will bless them because their religious leaders have given them valuable counsel; but, they only deceive themselves. On the other hand, power unbridled by law creates anarchy and despotism in the land.

In religion (i.e. law without power) the basis of right and wrong is settled through debates and arguments. Everyone tries to prove the supremacy and truthfulness of their religion through logic and philosophy. The Quran provides Permanent Values (immutable laws) for whose implementation power and authority are indispensable.

Government (Political power)

---

[3] Iron meaning power; an allusion to force of arms since iron/steel formed the material for swords, the weapon representative of force

The power to implement these values is known as *Istakhlaf* (government). The *Deen* is established through *Istakhlaf.*

> Allah has promised such of you as believe (in His revelation with reason and knowledge) and do good deeds (in order to accept the responsibility of governance) that He will surely make them to succeed (the present rulers) in the land just as He caused to succeed (others) those who were before them; and that He will surely establish in authority and power their *Deen* which He has approved for them, and that He will change (their state), after the fear in which they (lived), to one of security and peace so that they remain obedient and subservient only to Him. Those who reject (the Divine laws) henceforth, they are the miscreants (who spread rebellion and disorder in earth). (24:55)

What, then, is the result of establishing the *Deen*? Man does not associate anyone with the Authority of Allah and remains obedient and subservient *(ibada)* only to Him. In this way the laws enshrined in the Quran would be implemented and the power thus achieved would be accountable to the laws of Allah. The Quran and the sword (wisdom and power) are inseparable. In other words, to make the teachings of the Quran practically applicable one needs power which should be guided by the teachings of the Quran.

About this power the Quran states:

> O Muslim, keep ready what force you can muster to meet your enemy together with strong cavalry with which you can strike terror in the hearts of those who are enemy to Allah and to you; and those beside them whom you do not know but whom Allah knows. (8:60)

This, however, does not mean that the *Deen* given by Allah and enshrined in the Quran would be established by the power of the sword. People would not be forced to become Muslims. We have already stated in detail that forcing a person to become, or remain Muslim, is against the basic fundamentals of the Quran. Now the question arises: What is the purpose of this power? The following chapter proposes to present its answer.

2
POWER

In the last chapter we saw that:

- Man is a social animal. Collective life (society) is essential for his survival.
- Forming and establishing a society is known as State.
- A State requires a system.
- The establishment and stabilization of this system is based on power.
- The various types of States proposed by man are all based on the principle that some people have the right to rule over others and also draft laws for them.
- Manmade laws are based on the requirements of governance and not on human ethics.
- Moral laws are given by religion, which is based on worship of God or some other deity.
- Politics is separated from religion and both remain unrelated.
- Islam presents a system of State in which Allah is the Central Authority and only He is the Sovereign, and the State is the means and the medium to implement the laws of Allah.

In this context the first question is: how would such a State be established? We have seen that there is no compulsion in Islam. *Eiman* is to ponder over the Divine facts with patience. If in the light of reason and knowledge these facts appeal to the heart and intellect they should be accepted for their verity and adopted as the ideal goal of life. In this way the people believing in the truth of the Quran form one community. When this community becomes formidable, it will formulate a system of State in which the realities, on which its members believed with reason and knowledge, will become the code of their practical life. In other words, these facts will take the form of laws and constitution.

But so far the role of power has not been mentioned. Obviously in any State power is required to police the culprits. So this is the first stage where this State will need power.

This State will certainly also have non-Muslim residents. The State shall be responsible for protecting their lives, belongings, religion, places of worship and honour. Power will be required for this protection. It is also possible that these people might try to rebel against the State. Again, power is needed to defend the State.

Jihad and qitaal

Besides, it is also possible that other States put hindrances in the formation of this new State or they try to attack and destroy it after it has been formed. So, power is needed to defend the State; and the act of defence might escalate into a full-fledged war.

So for the establishment, stability and existence of a Quranic State, regular struggle and strife is required. Subsequently, a situation might arise when armed combat becomes inevitable. The Quran has used the word *jihad* for regular struggle and strife, whereas for armed combat the term used is *qitaal*. This shows that though *qitaal* is also a part of *jihad*, every act of *jihad* (struggle) is not *qitaal* (armed combat/war). Those who overlook this difference, deliberately or unknowingly use the word *jihad* for *qitaal*. And, since the Quran has laid a lot of emphasis on *jihad*, [1] their propaganda is, "Look the Quran at every step instigates a Muslim to wage Holy War against infidels."

It would be interesting to note as to precisely when and under what circumstances armed combat was first allowed by the Quran. The last Messenger began his mission in Mecca and started forming the Muslim community. At that time there was no question of using force. *Deen* was presented through logic and reasoning. People accepted it whole-heartedly after pondering over its principles. But the Quraish (the local Meccans, the tribe of the Prophet) opposed the mission of the last Messenger vehemently. When this opposition reached dangerous proportions, the Messenger migrated to Medina where the atmosphere was conducive for the establishment of the *Deen*. But, even there the Quraish did not allow the Messenger and his followers to live in peace.

---

1 In the Quranic scheme of things, the life of a Muslim consists of *jihad* [struggle] from cradle to the grave

They marched towards Medina with a large contingent of armed men. Now, the Muslims had just two options: get killed by the Quraish, or to make a last effort for their survival in the battlefield. Allah approved of the latter option for them. That was the first time the Muslims were allowed to participate in a war.

> To those (Muslims) against whom war is waged, permission is given (to fight), because they have been wronged, and Allah is indeed able to give them help; (they are) those who have been expelled from their homes in defiance of right- (for no cause) except that they say, "Only Allah is our Sustainer." (22:39-40)

The Quran goes on to state:

> (They are) those who, if We give them power in the land, establish *Salaat* (the political system of Islam) and provide to human beings the means and resources of development, enjoin the right and forbid the wrong. All their affairs would be decided in accordance with the laws of Allah. (22:41)

These verses clearly show as to when and why the Muslims were allowed to take up arms. This principle should always be kept in mind that Islam is the strongest advocate of religious freedom in the world. It allows religious freedom to every community of the world and it is obligatory on the Muslim community to protect this freedom. Since it guarantees religious freedom to every community, it has the right to safeguard its own freedom.

When 'the sword' (arms) is to be used

To religions other than Islam religious freedom incorporates nothing more than the liberty to perform the acts of worship and religious rituals. Muslims will, of course, accord this freedom to all. But, to them, this is only a small part of their *Deen*, religious freedom being much more than that. Their *Deen* encompasses every aspect of human life. Therefore, according to their *Deen,* 'religious freedom' means functioning of their system of State in complete independence without hindrance or interference from others. Muslims will thwart all efforts aimed at obstructing and disturbing the formation of their system or conspiring to destroy it. Initially, Muslims will try to resolve the matter through dialogue and treaties employing peaceful methods. If these efforts fail and the oppressive forces do not mend their ways and, intoxicated by power and wealth, keep on violating human values, Muslims, armed with swords, shall enter the battlefield where they will either win freedom for their *Deen* or become martyrs. To a Muslim it is a thousand times better to die while defending the Truth than to live in a system opposed to the laws of Allah.

A Muslim never wants to be a slave to another man. He will not breathe in the polluted atmosphere of a system that does not run in accordance to the laws of Allah. From a worldly point of view such a system might offer him unlimited guarantee of peace and security but he is not going to accept it. For him the definitions of 'peace' and 'disorder' are entirely different. If a government forcefully crushes robbery, looting, violence, etc. and thereby the populace can live in peace and security in their homes and can travel safely, it is considered a peaceful regime because there is no disorder and evil under its jurisdiction. Surely, Islam too is against disorder and evil. But it goes beyond this. According to Islam the real peace and security lies in the fact that Man remains slave only to Allah and not to any human being so as to receive felicity and prosperity in this life and in the Hereafter. This system of State is called *Haq* (Truth). Apart from this, all other systems are *batil* (False). Disorder occurs when *Haq* is made subservient to *batil* or, in other words, the system of State is not in accordance with the Divine laws. The Quran states:

> And if the Truth had followed their desires, verily there would have been disorder in the heavens and the earth and all being therein. We are saying that the Truth should not be subservient to human desires because it is for their own benefit and dignity. But their attitude is so wrong that they turn away from their own honour and respect. (23:71)

Therefore, the Quran specifically states that:

> Those who believe (in the laws of Allah with reason and knowledge) fight in the cause of Allah (so as to establish His system). On the contrary, those who reject (the Divine revelation) fight for the cause of ungodly authorities. So those who believe should fight the friends of Satan (without fearing their power and resources). Remember that in the face of the Truth feeble indeed is the cunning of Satan. (4:76)

Permission for War

In the above verse difference between a *Momin* (Believer) and a *Kafir* (Non-believer) is clearly marked. Those who fight in the way of Truth so as to establish the Kingdom of Allah are *Momineen.* And those who fight to establish any other system are *Kafireen.* As such, when people or States create obstructions in the establishment of the system of Allah and conspire to destroy it, and all peaceful methods have been exhausted to stop them, it is permissible for Muslims to take up arms against them. These were the circumstances when for the first time Muslims were allowed to 'unsheathe the sword'. Let us ponder once again over the verse that gives permission to participate in a war.

> To those (Muslims) against whom war is waged, permission is given (to fight), because they have been wronged, and Allah is indeed able to give them help; (they are) those who have been expelled from their homes in defiance of right- (for no cause) except that they say, "Only Allah is our Sustainer." Did not Allah check one set of people by means of another, there would surely have been pulled down monasteries, churches, synagogues, and mosques, in which the name of Allah is commemorated in abundance, Allah will certainly aid those who aid his (cause); for verily Allah is full of strength, exalted in might. (22:39-40)

The details and exposition of this can be found at various places in the Quran.

> (The fundamental principle is that) you should only fight those who aggress against you and leave you no option but to fight; do not initiate hostilities. This war will be in the way of Allah i.e. for the protection of humanity from tyranny and oppression. But even in this war the limits of law must not be transgressed, for such transgression is against the laws of Allah, and Allah does not like transgressors. (2:190)

At another place the Quran states:

> You should fight your enemies until you have dissipated the mischief they have caused, and created an environment where no compulsion or oppression is exercised in matters of *Deen.* But

> when you see that your enemies have given up the mischief, you should cease to fight them (because the purpose of war is to prevent forces of oppression and lawlessness from spreading and once this purpose is achieved there is no need for further warfare). (2:193)

It has already been stated that the Quran is the biggest guarantor and advocate of religious freedom in the world. This freedom also includes the right to preach and propagate your religion with the condition that the feelings of the followers of other religions are not hurt and the motive is not to further political cause. Besides, deceitful methods of preaching should not be adopted. The Quran wants this type of freedom accorded to its followers as well.

Honouring Treaties

The Islamic State will enter into treaties of peace and security with other nations. And if any nation violates these treaties, under certain circumstances war would become inevitable. Honouring of treaties is a fundamental teaching of the Quran. According to the Quran, those who violate this principle are grave offenders. It charges the Jews with violating this principle and history testifies that they always did so:

> (And today those who are rejecting the Truth have always been in the habit of breaking promises). Whenever their representatives make an agreement on behalf of the entire community, it is repudiated by some of them who regard the agreement as a piece of waste paper. This is because most of them have no faith in the Divine laws. (2:100)

The Quran states that those who reject the laws of Allah are also guilty of violating this principle.

> So far are they from adhering to the terms of the treaties made with the Divine Order, they do not even respect their ties of relationship with the believers. These are the people who have transgressed beyond all limits (of social and political behaviour). (9:10)

The attitude of the Muslims is in total contradiction to this. When they enter into agreement with anyone they fulfil it (2:177), because the

Quran orders them to honour their treaties and promises (5:1). This basic principle of honouring treaties is frequently mentioned in the Quran:

> You should always fulfill your commitments. (Since you make Allah your Guarantor therefore) every commitment should be fulfilled because every agreement will be enquired into. (17:34)

And:

> And when you enter into agreement with each other, fulfill it (because your agreement becomes a covenant with Allah). And break not your oaths after you have confirmed them; indeed you have made Allah your surety; for Allah knows all that you do. (16:91)

Sublime Heights

In this context the Quran takes man to such sublime heights that astonish even a prudent man. Let us suppose that the Islamic State has entered into a treaty with a nation. But Muslims in that nation are being persecuted and therefore ask the Islamic State for help. What should the Islamic State do? Abrogate the treaty? No. The Quran does not permit that because that would amount to violating a permanent value, i.e. honour one's commitments.

And those who have believed, yet not left their homes to join the Divine Order, though they had the opportunity to do so, they shall have no right of protection from you until they too leave their homes. However, if they seek aid from you in the matter of *Deen* it will be obligatory on you to provide it except if the aid goes against those with whom you have a treaty. Remember that Allah watches your actions. (8:72)

Betrayal is Prohibited

It is essential for Muslims to keep their word as long as their opponents also honour the terms of an agreement that they might have entered into. But if there are logical reasons to believe that the opponents are likely to violate the treaty, Muslims have the right to nullify the treaty. Nevertheless they are not allowed to betray their opponents. Any abrogation of the treaty has to be announced openly and unambiguously.

(O Muslims) if you fear treachery at the hands of those with whom you have a treaty, do not break the treaty unilaterally but tell the other side that the treaty will not be binding on you any more. In this way, both the parties will be on equal ground. Remember Allah does not like the treacherous. (8:58)

If we compare this teaching with the faiths and ways of the political world, the difference is self-evident. According to an ancient lawmaker: [2]

Treaty is a spider's web which entangles the one who is weaker than it, and it is not worth more than a straw for the one who is stronger than the web.

The modern political world seems to be influenced by the Italian thinker, Machiavelli. Let us see what he states in this context:

A prince being thus obliged to know well how to act as a beast must imitate the fox and the lion, for the lion cannot protect himself from traps and the fox cannot defend himself from wolves. One must, therefore, be a fox to recognise traps, and a lion to frighten wolves. Those that wish to be only lions do not understand this. Therefore, a prudent ruler ought not to honour a treaty when it is no longer beneficial and when the original reasons no longer exist. [3]

The entire edifice of Western politics and civilisation is constructed on the basis of Machiavellian philosophy [3]. Consequently, in the modern political world of today treaties and agreements are not honoured though it claims to be a champion of human welfare and prosperity and a surety of justice and impartiality. The leaders of Western civilisation are quite adept in breaking their promises with the most unscrupulous impudence and audacity. They violate treaties and agreements in no time. They do not hesitate in doing so because to them 'wrong' and 'right' are synonymous; treachery and betrayal do not amount to immorality. The fundamental principle of Machiavellian thought is that moral considerations are irrelevant to political affairs.

---

[2] Solon, Greek philosopher & poet, c. 638 BC–558 BC

[3] R. Briffault, *The Making of Humanity*, Ch. 18

Only success matters in politics. How it is achieved is immaterial. States the prophet of Satanic politics, Machiavelli, "Means are justified by the ends achieved." His followers are following this in letter and spirit. As a result, along with themselves they have forced the rest of the world into the hell of destruction.

How were agreements and treaties treated when the last Messenger came on the stage of the world? This question will be answered a little later. Here, it is suffice to say that the Islamic State will enter into treaties with non-Muslim nations and it will be obligatory on it to honour those treaties. But conflict with a treacherous nation would be imperative. This is the third reason for war. The last Messenger entered into agreements with his Arab opponents but they regularly went back on their promises.

> Mark this: the worst of creatures in Allah's sight are those who will never believe in His laws. (O Messenger, your opponents are similar to these creatures). You had made a treaty with them, which they have violated repeatedly without realizing or fearing as to what the results of this would be. (8:55-56)

As such war against them became imperative. Read the first two sections of the ninth chapter of the Quran. You will become acquainted with the details of the treacheries of these people.

Treachery

These people were so strongly opposed to Islam that they even violated their age-old conventions and customs. They had a long-established custom of observing four months of a year as sacred during which fighting was forbidden and everyone was allowed to go about their business in peace. The sacredness of these months was maintained even through any mutual conflicts. The Quran carried this tradition on and duly ordered its followers against violating the sanctity of these months. But the treachery of the enemies of Islam reached such blatant heights that they changed the sacred months when it suited them and tried to get an unfair advantage over their opponents.

> Indeed the transposing (of a month in which war is forbidden) is an addition to *kufr* (rejecting the Divine laws). Such intercalation (amounts to violating the treaties and the international laws and) is but one more instance of their refusal to acknowledge the

> Truth. Their rejection of the Truth has led them astray. For they declare a month to be sacred one year, and forbidden another year, in order to agree with the number of month forbidden by Allah and make such forbidden ones lawful. The gains that accrue to them in this way seem very fair to them; but Allah does not grace with His guidance people who refuse to acknowledge the Truth. (9:37)

This is the worst form of treachery and the Quran calls it "an addition to *kufr* (rejecting the laws of Allah)."

War against Oppression

Owing to the preaching and propagation of Islam people in other nations might also become Muslims. If any nation is violent against such new entrants to the way of Allah then it is the responsibility of the Islamic State to help and protect them. In such circumstances if efforts of peace and negotiations fail, war becomes essential.

> (O Muslims) what is the matter with you that you do not fight in the cause of Allah? Do you not hear the cries of helpless and oppressed men, women and children? They are crying: "O our Sustainer! Rescue us from this town, of which the people are oppressors. Give us from Thy presence some protecting friend. Give us from Thy presence some defender." (4:75)

If oppressors and their acts of tyranny and oppression are not prevented, the weak will have no life. Therefore, the Quran orders Muslims to help the oppressed.

> Remember, those who reject the Divine Order and those who are oppressors are friends to one another. If you do not act against them as directed by Allah, there will be disorder, chaos and corruption in the land. (8:73)

Though these verses are in context of the people of Mecca but are applicable universally. This means that it is the duty of the soldiers of Allah to protect the oppressed irrespective of their religion, community, colour, race and nation. The mission of life of these soldiers is to maintain the honour of humanity and in this process they can even lay down their lives. If no one stands up for the weak and the oppressed, this world will become a predators' den. We are already witnessing that, owing to the highhandedness of the West, there is no peace and safety for the powerless in this vast land of Allah. Hence the Quranic orders to defend the weak:

> And if Allah did not check one group of people by means of another; the earth would indeed be full of mischief and disorder (there would not have been peace and justice). In this way the checking of the oppressive forces is Allah's boon to all peoples. (2:251)

Mediator

We should consider one more scenario in this regard: two individuals are fighting with each other on the road, a policeman sees and arrests them, takes them to the court of law, and the guilty is punished. But if two nations are at war with each other, who is going to police them? Which court is going to hear their case and punish the erring nation? In fact there is disorder in the entire world because there is no police and no court to stop and punish the erring nations. After the First World War the exhausted nations formed the 'League of Nations" in order to reach this objective. But all the participants in this League did not mean well. The honeymoon was short-lived and the result was the Second World War. After this, the 'United Nations' was formed. It does not take an astrologer to predict that this will also meet the same fate because its basis is no different from that of the 'League of Nations'. The fact is that this problem can only be solved by the Quranic sagacity. Only the Quran has given the idea of such a forum. Europe borrowed this idea from the Quran but it ignored the spirit that makes such a forum work. Only the laws of Allah can do it. In the Satanic politics of the West Allah is an object of hate. The spirit of Satan cannot produce results that the laws of Allah guarantee. It is the duty of the soldiers of Allah to become mediators in all disputes and conflicts in the world. Their decisions should be in accordance with justice and fairness, and whichever party violates their just decision so as to spread disorder and mischief, should be crushed. Therefore, the Quran states to Muslims:

> Thus We (Allah) have made you a community with a universal outlook to be equidistant from all other communities i.e. neither leaning towards any particular people nor estranged from another. Your responsibility is to keep a watch over the activities

> of other people of the world (to see that no nation oppresses another) and the responsibility of the Messenger (being the head of the State) is to keep watch over your activities. (2:143)

Punishment for Rebellion

These are the circumstances in which the Quran allows Muslims to wage war. Apart from these, there are two or three other conditions that pertain to the internal management of the Islamic State. The Quran allows an individual to change his religion if he loses faith in the laws of Allah. But it does not allow a person to rebel against the Divine Order while remaining a member of the Muslim community. The decisions of the system of State are law and every resident of a State must be law-abiding; it cannot be optional. A system can only survive if its laws are followed. There are two ways of violating laws: one, a person believes that the laws are correct but he/she violates them for one reason or another. Such a person would be considered an Accused and will be tried in a court of law and, if proven guilty, would be punished; two, a person rebels against the (State) system. This, according to the Quran, is war against Allah and His Messenger. A grave penalty is suggested for this crime.

> The punishment of those who wage war against Allah and His Messenger, and strive with might and main for mischief and disorder through the land, is execution, or crucifixion, or the cutting off of hands and feet from opposite sides, [4] or exile from the land: that is their disgrace in this world, and a heavy punishment is their lot in the Hereafter. (5:33)

Hypocrisy

Much more serious than rebellion is another situation which produces grave results: an individual is apparently a member of the Muslim community and outwardly appears to be abiding by its laws, but secretly works against it and also conspires with others for its destruction. This behaviour is known as hypocrisy.

The Quran has repeatedly warned the Hypocrites to mend their ways; they should either accept Islam whole-heartedly or reject it openly.

---

[4] *Cutting off of hands and feet from opposite sides* is an allegorical expression for arresting and sending to prison.

But, if they ignore both these options and continue with their conspiracies so as to harm Islam, war is allowed to crush them. No government can tolerate such elements.

> O Messenger! Strive hard against the *kafreen* (rejecters) and the *munaafeqeen* (hypocrites). Be strict with them (because the treacheries of the Rejectors and conspiracies of the Hypocrites have crossed limits of tolerance). Their ultimate destination is hell (of destruction), which is a very trying destination. (9:73)

War to End War

These are the circumstances in which the Quran has allowed the Muslims to participate in war. However, what must be kept in mind is that this permission is given only till war itself lays down its burden.

> Therefore, when you (O Muslims) meet (in fight) those who oppose the Divine Order, smite at their necks; at length, when you have thoroughly subdued them, bind (the captives) firmly: (as for the prisoners of war) either (release them with) generosity or ransom. (You should continue your struggle) till the war itself lays down its burden. (4:4)

3
WAR

In the previous chapter we have already discussed the circumstances in which the Quran permits war. In this context there is nothing new to add save one aspect.

Objections against War

One school of thought believes that whatever the circumstances, war in any case is a barbarity and madness and it cannot be justified, let alone permitted. It is the law of the jungle, a reminder of the time in human history when conflicts were settled by brutal force and not by reason and evidence. Therefore, in the present age of intellect and knowledge, and also of culture and civilisation, it cannot be allowed even as the last resort. It is against human dignity to force men to accept a particular point of view; Men have been endowed with intellect and culture and should settle their conflicts and disputes by negotiations. War is a brutal act. Love, peace, harmony, accord, mercy are all jewels of humanity. Fire and blood destroy them. Well, on paper this teaching appears to be very appealing, balanced and humane. And those who oppose this teaching are always considered cruel and cold–hearted. But the question is: does this teaching appear good only in the world of words or, can it be implemented in practice?

Christian Viewpoint

In the Old Testament orders for war are unambiguously listed. A major portion of this Scripture is devoted to wars fought by the Children of Israel. For instance, see chapter 13 in the Book of Numbers. Therefore, Jews cannot object to war. Christianity pretends to be the biggest champion of anti-war philosophy. The New Testament states

'Do not resist him that is wicked; but whoever slaps you on your right cheek, turn the other also to him.'[1]

Therefore, let us look at Christianity first. In my book *Shola-e-Mastoor* (The Hidden Flame) I have discussed the life and teachings of Jesus Christ in detail. I have said that Jesus did not preach cowardice. This element was introduced into Christianity by St. Paul at the time when Christians were in hopeless circumstances and, as the survivors of a revolutionary community, they were being charged with rebellion. Consequently, this teaching was evolved in order to save them from the oppressive and tyrannical government of the day. Thus a philosophy detrimental to Man's freedom and self-respect became part of Christianity.

Evidence from Christians

How much has this philosophy damaged humanity?

Non-Muslim philosophers and historians who have objectively studied history have answered this question. The German philosopher Nietzsche was of the opinion that Christianity has always supported the weak, downtrodden and rotten elements of society. Its aim is to eradicate all self-respecting intellectual prowess of Man. Highly intellectualised brains have been destroyed by it.

But, in the second volume of his history of European morality, he writes that Christianity gave birth to humility and lowliness; and these qualities remained appropriate and suitable for quite a considerable period. But this philosophy of humility could not keep pace with rapid development of culture till the end. For progress and civilisation it is essential that a community should have the mindset for self-respect and freedom. Humility and lowliness are counter-progressive.

G. A. Dorsey, the famous historian of civilisations, has asserted that today millions of people feel that Christianity is the religion of the defeated. They accept the religion and thus admit solemnly its defeatist spirit. "Nothing is satisfactory in life", they argue. "Desire for satisfaction is wrong and satisfaction of wrong desires is sin" is a slogan which makes a true and healthy life impossible. It destroys humanity.[2]

---

[1] Matthew 5:39 (New World Translation)

[2] G.A. Dorsey, *Civilisation*, p.446

"Love your enemies," is an order which is impossible to implement. W. A. Brend writes in his book *Foundation of Human Conflicts* that the order of the New Testament to love your enemies is a psychological impossibility. Samuel Lowy has echoed similar thoughts in his book *Man and Fellow Man.* And the writer of *Civilisation, War and Death,* Sigmund Freud states that the order to love thy enemies is a practical impossibility. Such lofty ideals of love cannot eradicate Evil. Culture does not care for such orders. It is easy to utter this sacred order but quite difficult to follow it. [3]

"Do not resist him that is wicked" is such an order that if it is followed, all the forces of Evil in the world would be free to operate and oppression, injustice, tyranny and hardship would overpower every aspect of social and civilised life. For this reason Robert Briffault levels the grave charge against Christianity that with this wrong teaching it has always supported cruelty and oppression and in this way did away with justice and fairness. In *The Making of Humanity* he quotes the Spanish scholar, Dr. Falta de Gracia, as having stated:

> The notion of justice is as entirely foreign to the spirit of Christianity as is that of intellectual honesty. It lies wholly outside the field of its ethical vision.

Dr. Gracia further states that Christianity has been sympathetic to the oppressed people but has always forgiven cruelty and oppression. It has invited those oppressed people to the path of love who have been engrossed with difficulties and problems from all sides. It teaches them a lesson of forgiveness and pardon. It has reminded them that God is the Sustainer. But in this mayhem of religion and morality there is no scope for justice and probity. Christianity has painted a picture in which the angel-like sacred Christ descends from the sky amongst the victims of oppression and tyranny, and gives them the blessed message of Paraclete. But it is beyond his message to find out the grounds of oppression and tyranny. He does not correctly contemplate the concept of Good and Evil. To him, this cruelty and oppression is a testing time for sinners. It is also a distinctive quality of his system; this is the verdict of "God's Kingdom on Earth". St. Vincent Francis visits a living hell of a prison. There, he preaches love and asks the inmates to repent. But he does not even think of the causes which created that hell-hole in the first place. Even when the victims of oppression and cruelty cry in pain, men remain

[3] S. Freud, *Civilisation, War and Death* pp. 78-94

in bondage, people bleed to death, the spirit of Christianity will only console them. But Christianity will not think of the ways of eradicating oppression and tyranny because it does not think it to be its responsibility. The spirit of Christianity has remained as unconcerned towards justice and fairness as to the idea of truth. It has always taught forgiveness, tolerance and mercy. But it never remembered justice and fairness. Christianity has been influenced by unnatural moral laws of "Do not resist him that is wicked", "love your enemies", "suppress your desires", "whoever slaps you on your right cheek, turn the other also to him", etc. but no scene of oppression and tyranny shook it. [4]

More Evidence

Evil and oppression can be resisted only by power which is prohibited in Christianity. Forces of tyranny and oppression can be arrested only by power. But in Christianity power is the right of Caesar and not God. Therefore the forces of Evil and oppression are free to do what they like. It is sinful for a victim to even think of revenge because the Kingdom is of Heaven and not of Earth. A victim has to love his oppressor because this is "an order from his God". With such an attitude on the part of theists, Evil will reign supreme in the world. We have already stated that it is impossible to follow commands such as "love your enemies" and "Do not resist him that is wicked". As such, today the thinkers and philosophers of Christianity are saying that sometimes circumstances may arise when war becomes inevitable. Dean Inge's comment on this way of combating evil deserves careful consideration. He states:

> The principle of non-resistance was laid down for a little flock in a hostile environment. But an organised society cannot abstain from the use of coercion. No one would suggest that Christian Government must not suppress a gang of criminals within its own borders, and if this is admitted, can we doubt that it should defend itself against an invading enemy? …….. Augustine held that war is justified in repelling wanton and rapacious attacks and that in preventing such crimes we are acting in the true interest of the aggressor. Without justice, what is an empire but brigandage on a large scale? Allowing that circumstances may arise which

[4] R. Briffault, *The Making of Humanity* pp. 322-333

make a defensive war inevitable, we have to find principles which will guide us practically. [5]

The Archbishop of Canterbury holds a very prominent position in the Church of England. According to the news agency *Reuters*, he said that circumstances might arise in which participation in war would not be against Christian principles. [6] Similar circumstances arose in the form of the Second World War. Sir Richard Gregory has drawn a very vivid picture of this. He states that the Church of Christ blessed the Forces and their arms and it is another matter that every Christian State that took part in the war asked for help from the same God. [7]

These quotations totally reject the claim of the Christian missionaries that they oppose war because it is against culture and humanity and the message of Christianity is protest against war. Why do Christian missionaries propagate this teaching? The answer to this question would be given a little later.

Hindu Religion and War

Hinduism is a religion of war and violence. Like the Old Testament the Vedas are also full of stories pertaining to wars. They narrate the exploits of Aryans and how they conquered the non-Aryans. Besides, the Vedas also contain accounts of wars fought by their *devta*'s (gods). Rig Veda states that god Indra "killed Wartara and destroyed villages and towns, will also destroy the black Dravidians". [8] At another location the same Veda states that he (Indra) killed and destroyed fifty thousand black Dravidians in the battle. [9] For details of these wars one can go through *The Ancient Civilisation of India* by R. C. Dutt.

Furthermore, Ram and Krishna appear in Hindu history as incarnations of God. *Ramayana* and *Mahabharta* are considered sacred religious books. *Ramayana* narrates the tale of the war that Ram fought against Ravana, the king of Lanka (Sri Lanka, previously Ceylon). Mahabharata gives an account of the war fought between cousins Kauravs and Pandavs. This epic also contains *Geeta.* In this war Krishna

---

[5] R. W. Inge, *The Fall of the Idols* p. 179-181

[6] Reuters: *Nation Calls* 22 December 1936

[7] R. Gregory, Religion in Science and Civilisation, p. 274

[8] Rig Veda, Mandal 2, Mantra 20, Richa 607

[9] Ibid. 4/16/10

was the charioteer of Arjun. But, once they are on the battlefield, Arjun develops cold feet and does not want to fight against his own relatives. But Krishna preaches to him the desirability of war. Thus *Geeta* is essentially Krishna's sermon in favour of war to Arjun in the battlefield. Such, then, are the exploits of Ram and Krishna on the basis of which they are considered to be incarnations of God.

Philosophy of Mahatma Gandhi …

With this backdrop it is improbable for a Hindu to oppose the concept of war. But the Hindu religion accepts all kinds of contradictory thoughts. Therefore, it is being said that Hinduism preaches *ahimsa* (non-violence) and consequently it is *parmo dharam*, or the best religion. The political leader of the Hindu community, Mahatma Gandhi, is propagating this theory of ahimsa. [10] What political gains does he want to make from this? The answer to this question is irrelevant to the theme of this book. However, the relevant question is: does the theory of *ahimsa* have the potential to be applicable in all circumstances and in every section of human life?

By *ahimsa* it is meant that one should not harbour the feeling of revenge, should not use violence to resist evil, and should not resort to violence whatever the circumstances. According to Mahatma Gandhi, *ahimsa* is the Truth. And for this reason he has been speaking in its favour for the last twenty to twenty-five years. But circumstances did arise in which the Mahatma himself advised against *ahimsa.*

… and his Confession

In an issue of *Harijan* dated 9 August 1946 there was a report that a white man insulted an African priest. Though the priest was much stronger and healthier than the white man still he said: "Please forgive me." the Mahatma's comment on this incident was that this was not ahimsa. This was an insult to the teachings of Christ. Courage demanded that the priest should have paid back in the same coin.

Similarly, regarding the communal riots in Calcutta in 1946, his editorial pronounced that:

---

[10] The Urdu original version of this book was written before 1947 when Gandhi's philosophy of *ahimsa* was at its peak in India. The translator has thus retained the use of the present tense.

> They (the victims) can retaliate or refrain. Refraining is easy and simple, if there is the will. Retaliation is complicated. Will it be tooth against or many against one? [11]

Regarding the sanctity of life, the Mahatma believes that snakes, scorpions, wolves and similar beasts and reptiles that are harmful to man should be killed. Responding to objections, he said that it is impossible for a man to avoid violence completely. Now, the question is where to draw the demarcation line? For every man it would be different. After this he writes that on the basis of *ahimsa* animals cannot be allowed to destroy the crop and that too when there is draught in the country. This is sin. Good and evil are relative things. A thing good in one particular condition might become evil in the other. [12]

This shows that according to the Mahatma *ahimsa* is a relative truth and not absolute truth; and circumstances might arise when following *ahimsa* becomes a sin. Sometimes *himsa* (violence) becomes a virtue. This is exactly what Islam teaches. According to Islam, in some situations, forgiveness and pardon are virtues and in some the Mosaic staff is justice and truth. In this context the Mahatma writes at another place that monkeys create nuisance and inflict loss. People get utterly sick of them and desire that they should die. When someone kills them these people feel joy in their heart but overtly they oppose the killing of monkeys. One friend, who is well-versed in Scriptures, asks as to what *ahimsa* states about monkeys that destroy crops and whose population is on the increase?

In answer to the above question the Mahatma writes:

> My ahimsa is my own. I am not able to accept in its entirety the doctrine of non-killing of animals. I have no feeling in me to save the lives of animals which devour or cause hurt to man. I consider it wrong to help in the increase of their progeny. Therefore, I will not feed ants, monkeys or dogs. I will never sacrifice a man's life in order to save theirs. Thinking along these lines I have come to the conclusion that to do away with monkeys where they have become a menace to the wellbeing of man is pardonable. Such killing becomes a duty. The

---

[11] *Harijan* 25 August 1946.; *Collected Works of Mahatma Gandhi* (hereinafter referred to as *CWMG*) Vol. 92 p.45

[12] See *Harijan*, 9 June 1946; *CWMG* Vol. 91, p.61-62

question may arise as to why this rule should not also apply to human beings. It cannot because, however bad, they are as we are. Unlike the animal, man has been given the faculty of reason. [13]

Weak Argument

The last portion of the above quotation deserves attention. If any person, or a group, imitates wolves and monkeys and destroys crops, creates disorder and chaos in the land so that there is danger to life, property, freedom, women's honour, and any peaceful reasoning on humanitarian grounds against these acts is answered by violence, what should be done in such a situation? Should they be left alone to increase their nefarious activities? Should they be not stopped forcibly just because are human beings? If the answer to these questions is in the positive then no system can remain in peace and security. There is no doubt that knowledge and intellect are precious jewels by which only human beings have been blessed. But don't we observe daily that a person overcome by emotions, despite the gift of knowledge and intellect, commits crimes worst than animals would commit? The fact is that a person carried away by emotions and passions is no different from an inebriated one. Neither can see logic and reason. One can argue that dacoits and robbers are low in intellect. But what has happened to the intellect and wisdom of cultured and civilised communities of today? Almost on daily basis they are at loggerheads with each other. The memories of the Second World War are still fresh. For six long years these cultured and civilised peoples had turned this world into a hell of fire and blood and no logic or reason could stop them from committing their gruesome act. There is no doubt that, with proper upbringing, animal instinct in humans can be tamed. (That, precisely, is the objective of believing in, and following, Divine laws). But as long as such men in whom animal instinct is dominant exist, the 'rod of Moses', apart from reason, is required to protect humanity from these man-like beasts. About these beasts of men, the Quran states that they look like men but in reality they are worse than beasts. In this context the philosophers of Europe have also pondered much. They have also come to the conclusion that intellectual reasoning cannot stop war. Dean Inge observes:

> By and large the contemporary man is not militant but it is easy to infuse anger in him'. If this observation is correct, the

---

13 *Harijan*, 5 May 1946; *CWMG* Vol. 90 p.310

possibility of stopping war with logic and reasoning is quite remote. [14]

Similarly, H. L. Mencken, the author of *Treatise on Right and Wrong*, writes:

> Amidst the grim conspiracy of pitting one nation against another appear those ideological interests that dream of putting an end to war. If, by some miracle, their desire is fulfilled, the idol of Nationalism will meet its doom and many wrong and immoral things will go along with it. The source of the power of Nationalism lies in fear and no person will fear that enemy who is armed with the weapon of justice. But the chances of war coming to an end before the end of this contemporary period are very remote. And centuries might go by before this dream is realised. Man is still quite like barbaric jungle-folk. Besides, man is not ready to forgo the pleasure that he gets when, in a fit of anger, he goes in pursuit of his enemy or fights with him. The proposals of peace put forward by different governments are in fact requisitions of their interests.
>
> These observations are based on first hand knowledge that I got by attending three international conferences that were organised to end war. After hypocritical peace of a few days, the leaders participating in the conferences resorted to grabbing and scrambling. And, when they returned to their respective countries their success was not measured by what they did for restoring peace in the world but by what material they brought for future wars. The League of Nations disintegrated when its aims became known; only after a short period of its inception this thing came out into the open. Despite all the fictional claims that were made by its founders, the fact is that their aim was merely to ensure that the war booty of the World War remained with the victorious. And the moment this business started the victorious nations were in conflict with each other over the division of the war booty. [15]

We should recall that in 1932 Professor Einstein, under the auspices of the League of Nations' National Institute of Intellectual

---

[14] . Inge, op. cit., p.193

[15] H.L. Mencken, *Treatise on Right and Wrong* p.233

Cooperation, invited various thinkers of the West to answer the question: Is there a way to save humanity from war?

Responding to this question Sigmund Freud, the famous psychoanalyst, writes:

> Though this will appear contradictory, the fact is that the path of achieving the desired goal of everlasting peace will be paved by war only. With war big nations would be developed and within their boundaries their central authority would make war impossible. There is only one sure way of ending war and that is to create with mutual understanding such a central authority whose decisions are final and binding on nations that happen to be in conflict of interests with each other. But, two things are required to achieve this goal; one, creation of a supreme court and two, the power to implement its decision. If latter is missing, the former will automatically become useless. However, the question is not to curb dominant forces of man but how to use them in fields other than war. [16]

Freud concludes by saying:

> Intellectuals hate war because their physical nature demands it.

These are the views of those who are considered luminaries of knowledge and intellect in the world and who claim to solve every problem with logic and reasoning. The fact is that, if it had been possible to control the oppressive forces by reasoning with them, Ram would not have gone to Lanka to kill Ravana and Krishna would not have supported war in the field of Krushetra. If verbal reasoning had the potential of solving the problem of war then Krishna would have argued with Kauravas to stop the war instead of inciting Arjun to fight. Therefore, as long as oppressive forces are operating in the world, force would be required to suppress their tyranny and to protect civilised humanity. For this reason the flag-bearer of *ahimsa*, Mahatma Gandhi had to say:

> Women of India should be taught the art of using weapons. This is preferable to leaving them in a condition where they feel

[16] S. Freud, op. cit., pp.87-93

helpless. Women should be encouraged to keep revolvers and knives on their person. [17]

Christian Missionaries

The West is always absorbed and entangled in harassing and weakening the spirit and force of Islam. Why? This we have already answered. To achieve this objective the missionaries of the Church play the role of a vanguard for the Christian army.

These missionaries of the Church come in the guise of considerate friends. Before leaving the shores of Europe, they urge their arms industry to carry on making weapons of warfare. [18] But, in the East they preach to the Muslims the Jesuit message of "God's Kingdom is for the weak and the poor", and "whoever slaps you on your right cheek, turn the other also to him because the Kingdom of God has become your destiny"; and "the kingdom of this earth is useless and to desire it is ignominy." History has shown that the Christian missionaries have been adopting this method for centuries. They come to Muslim countries and preach to them stories of God's Kingdom and consequently the kingdom on earth of the Muslims gets transferred to other hands; yes, the same Muslims about whom their Allah said:

> The believers without doubt have entered into a transaction with Allah, through the instrumentality of the Divine order, Who purchases their very persons and their worldly possessions in return for the blissful life of *janna* [Paradise]. They shall fight in the cause of Allah and slay and be slain and on the part of Allah the promise of *janna* is binding. Similar promises were also made in the Torah and the Injeel [the Bible] and are reiterated here in the Quran. Who is better than Allah in fulfilling promises? O

---

[17] *Harijan*, 27 October 1946. Translated from Urdu version of this book as original is not available. A similar statement was however recorded in *Hindustan Times* and is reproduced here: "He (Gandhi) would far rather see India's women trained to wield arms than that they should feel helpless. He knew, however, that arms were a poor weapon when it came to the matter of defending one's honour against odds. Honour knew no surrender to any power on earth." (*Hindustan Times*, 19 October 1946; CWMG Vol. 92 p.356)

[18] Christianity preached its doctrine and prepared for war together. This is not a new thing. The Christian clergy was instrumental in instigating the Crusades. A Christian Historian writes: "When the victorious armies of the Messenger of Arabia entered Jerusalem (during the reign of the Second Caliph) not a single non-Muslim was killed on the ground that he professed a different religion. But when centuries later the Christian Crusaders entered Jerusalem then no Muslim man, woman or child was left alive."

believers! Rejoice then on the bargain effected which is a great achievement. (9:111)

And owing to the influence of the Christian missionaries, Muslims came to believe that the prayer mat and rosary beads represent real wealth in life. They misinterpreted "contentment" and "trust in Allah", converted *Deen* into religion, consumed the opium of religion and now they are totally oblivious to the demands of *Deen*.

Sheep and Tiger (the beast & the prey)

Dr. Muhammad Iqbal in his narrative poem *Asrar-e-Khudi* (Secrets of Self) has included a thought provoking allegory about the religious leaders of the West: There lived a tiger in a jungle. The tiger harassed the sheep of that jungle. The sheep assembled together to think up a solution. A sheep, well-versed in the art of politics said, "Listen. All of us sheep combined are no match to a tiger. Therefore, we should drop the idea of becoming a tiger. Instead, we should try to change the tiger into a sheep." Consequently that sheep donned the attire of a mystic and tactfully preached to the tiger the ideology of self-denial:

I possess spiritual power.
I am an apostle sent by God to tigers.
I have come as light for the blind eye,
I have come to establish laws and give commandments.
Repent over your blameworthy deeds!
O plotters of evil, bethink yourselves of good!
Whoso is violent and strong is miserable:
Life's solidity depends on self-denial.
The spirit of the righteous is fed by fodder:
The vegetarian is pleasing unto God.
The sharpness of your teeth brings disgrace unto you:
And makes blinds your perception.
Paradise is for the weak alone,
Strength is but a means of perdition.
It is wicked to seek greatness and glory,
Penury is sweeter than princedom.

The sheep was successful in its mission. The tiger became its disciple and started living on grass and vegetables instead of meat. After some time, it began to lose its strength, swiftness and activeness and became weak, humble, spineless and a coward. It lost the sharpness of its teeth and the spark of its eyes. There were left no desires in its heart. It became like a mirror that has lost its quality of reflection. It lost all desire for making an effort, lost enthusiasm to be active and to be always on the move. Once the king of the jungle had now lost all authority, firmness, determination, command, dignity, wisdom and prosperity. Its once powerful clasp of claw became weak and it became lifeless as if it was already in its grave. Hundreds of ailments afflict the weak. As such, the tiger became disgruntled, dispirited and of vile nature. Owing to the spell of the sheep, the ever-vigilant tiger went into a slumber. Besides, "culture" was the name he gave to his disgraceful decline.

In India

When the British abolished Muslim rule in India, they feared that Muslims would return to their venturesome way of life. Therefore they applied their time-tested formula and herds of Christian missionaries started coming to India. They spread their network through the length and breadth of the country and started preaching to the Muslims the concept of "Kingdom of God". One outcome of this preaching was Mirza Ghulam Ahmad of Qadiyan. [19] He himself admitted that his movement was the product of the seed sowed by the British. Apart from his fabricated 'revelation' he also preached against the concept of *jihad.* He said:

> O Friends! Now abandon the idea of jihad
> From now on, religion prohibits battle and war.

The result of this versified propaganda was that Muslims began to feel embarrassed at the mere mention of *jihad.* Even the attitude of those who did not accept the prophethood of the Qadiyani became apologetic. They began to desire for a Quran that had no verses on *jihad.* But this was not possible. Therefore, they began to offer ridiculous interpretation of the verses related to *jihad*: they said that the verses about *jihad* were time-bound and related to the period when the world had not become cultured – a time of madness and barbarity. The *jihad* instructions were

[19] Mirza Ghulam Ahmad (1835-1908), a religious figure from Qadian, India, was the founder of the Ahmadiyya religious movement in Islam. He claimed to be the Second Coming of Christ, the Promised Messiah, and the Mahdi, as well as being the *mujaddid* (Religious Revivalist) of the 14th Islamic century. However, most Muslims have rejected his claims.

appropriate then because the Arabs were naturally militant: but now all these verses have been abrogated.

The Message of Iqbal

This conspiracy was at the verge of becoming victorious when, fortunately for the Muslim community, Sir Muhammad Iqbal arrived on the scene and presented the real teachings of the Quran to the world.

> Curse on the community is the leadership
> That is secretively disciple to Pharaoh's power [20]

And Iqbal asked the 'considerate friends'-

> To protect the pomp and presage of the Wrong
> Europe armed herself from head to toe.
> O supporter of the Church!, I ask thee
> Is war evil only in the West and not in the East?
> If thou art just, not pertinent is it that
> Europe were forgiven and Islam be called to account. [21]

The modern Muslim is indebted to Iqbal who unveiled before him the truth of the Quran. Now, with the strength of his faith, he is presenting to the world the message of the Quran and also the attributes of the man (Prophet Mohammad (PBUH)) to whom the Quran was revealed.

> O Heaven! Sprinkle dew on his tomb
> O Bloom! O Harvest! Guard that house. [22]

Buddhism and Jainism

There is no doubt that both Buddhism and Jainism have preached sanctity of life. But the question is: what have they contributed to human civilisation? Throughout history, Jainism has never been a dominant force. And even today it does not have an independent identity. Thanks

---

[20] From *Nafsiyaat e ghulaami* (Psyche of Bondage) in Iqbal's *Zarb e Kaleem.*

[21] From *Jihad* in Iqbal's *Zarb e Kaleem.*

[22] Iqbal in *Waaleda Marhooma ki Yaad mein* (In Memory of Blessed Mother) in his *Baang e Draa.*

to Emperors Ashoka and Kanishka Buddhism did make some progress. But it took only one Hindu onslaught to drive the Buddhists out of India. Today, they are not recognised even as a minority community in India. It happened because these religions and their philosophies advocate salvation for individual life and are not concerned with collective life. At the time when Christians also believed in this philosophy their condition was not dissimilar to the Buddhists and the Jains. Dean Inge states that on the individual as well as universal level Christianity was only a religious movement.

The state of the Hindu religion is also the same. Mahatma Gandhi writes:

> If I were a dictator, religion and State would be separate. I swear by my religion. I will die for it. But it is my personal affair. The State has nothing to do with it. The State would look after your secular welfare, health, communications, foreign relations, currency and so on, but not your or my religion. That is everybody's personal concern! [23]

Government and Power

We have already stated that Islam is not a religion; it is a *Deen* that includes both religion and government. Look at any government, at every step it has to fight a war. What is war? It is to make somebody to accept something by force. We see that governments have to use force on a regular basis. When a criminal breaches peace, the police is ordered to arrest them. The criminal and the police both make use of their power against each other. The stronger dominates the weaker. Often the criminal is killed in such an encounter. But if he is arrested alive, his power (weapons, etc.) is snatched from him. He is tried in the court of law and if proven guilty, he is punished. This punishment is again implemented by force. This is called establishing peace in the land and is the basic obligation of an organised government. So, force is being used at every step and no Christian mystic or Hindu saint opposes it. They bless a government that establishes peace in the land. But when, instead of one individual an entire nation or community starts looting people, the use of force (war) against them is considered madness and barbarity. This shows that this philosophy is defective and trivial.

---

[23] *Harijan*, 22 September 1946: Talk with a Christian Missionary. *Collected Works of Mahatma Gandhi*, Vol. 92 p.190.

Resisting Evil

The Quran contains eternal truths. Therefore, it does not get influenced by cheap emotions and give these types of superficial 'moral laws'. To resist Evil is the fundamental principle of the *Deen*. It states that all evil should be eradicated and resisted. [24]

> (O Messenger) repel evil (judiciously) with that which is best. (23:96)

The Quran accepts that some evils are committed inadvertently. Appealing to one's intellect and sagacity can resist this type of evils. This is called "resisting evil with good":

> The Muslim community) averts evil with good and keeps open for human welfare that which We have given to them. (28:54)

The Quran states that by 'resisting evil with good' even an enemy can become a friend:

> Nor can Goodness and Evil be equal. Repel (evil) with what is better then will he between whom and thee was hatred become, as he were thy friend and intimate. (41:34)

The Quran, however, does not negate human emotions and therefore it does not limit itself to the above instructions. It considers the other side of the coin also. It states that amongst the evildoers there are such persons who deliberately violate the laws. They do not listen to any reasoning and soft approach towards them makes them more extremist. This type of evil can only be arrested by force and deserve punishment becomes.

> (Sometimes a culprit has to be punished but always keep this in mind that) the punishment should be equal (in degree) to the crime. (42:40)

The Quran also states that use of force for, or in support of, the oppressed is not a crime.

---

[24] The elimination of wrong is the irreducible minimum of morality. (R. Briffault, *The Making of Humanity*.)

> You have no right to charge or question a person who defends (or take revenge) himself after he has suffered wrong. (42:41)

Use of force is a crime when it is used for oppression, transgression, cruelty, riots, etc.

> The blame is only against those who oppress men with wrongdoing and insolently transgress beyond through the land, defying right and justice for such there will be a chastisement grievous. (42:42)

As such, the Quran instructs Muslims to forgive and to pardon. But, along with this, punishment is also considered essential so as to maintain peace and justice. This punishment, when extended beyond individuals to nations or communities, is called war. These measures good if they are for protecting human rights but evil if they are used for personal interests.

This fact was most eloquently stated by the last Messenger. He was asked: one man fights for war booty, one person fights for fame, one person fights for bravery, one person fights for anger and revenge. Whose Jihad is right? He replied:

> *Wa man qatala litakuna kalimatal lahi hiyal uuliya fahua fii sabilillahi.*

> One who fights in order to ensure that Allah's law (of justice and fairness) reign supreme then his *jihad* is in the Way of Allah. (Sahih Bukhari)

4
JIHAD

According to Greek philosophers the universe is static. This belief resulted in stoicism which means that one should lead a quiet, inactive, monotonous, hermetic life; shun society, and not have any sense of the values or joys of human co-existence. This pessimistic philosophy withered the leaves, plucked the fruits and dried up the branches of the tree of humanity. When the Messenger of Islam began his mission, this philosophy was dominated the thinking minds of the world in various ways. The Quran contradicted this listless and destructive philosophy of life and said that the universe is not static; it is ever-expanding in which every particle is changing and moving forward so as to live. The name of this endeavour is *jihad.*

The Meaning of jihad

Jihad is the opposite of *qo'ood* (to sit idly without making an effort). This makes it clear that *jihad* means to be active, to struggle, to strive and to endeavour.

> Those of the Believers who sit still, other than those who have a (disabling) hurt are not on equality with those who strive and struggle in the way of Allah with their wealth and lives. Allah has conferred on those who strive and struggle with their wealth and lives a rank above the sedentary. To each Allah has promised well, but He has bestowed on those who strive a great reward above the sedentary. (4:95)

Therefore, *jihad* means action. Reading the Quran from start to finish, one finds *eiman* and action emphasised throughout. *Eiman* is 'to determine an objective; action means striving and struggling in order to obtain that objective. That is the *jihad* of a Muslim. It includes everything from the smallest chore to the ultimate sacrifice that a man can make. So, in order to crush the forces of oppression and tyranny, a Muslim is prepared to lay down his life if circumstances so demand. As such, *qital* (armed combat) is also included in *jihad*. This means that every *jihad* is not war. The life of a Muslim is *jihad* from birth to death because only by *jihad* is the glory of human evolution maintained and human personality developed.

> If any (Muslim) strives and struggles then he does it for the development of his own personality because Allah is free of all needs from all creation. (29:6)

And the ways to the destination of the caravan of Life are shown by *jihad*.

> And Allah would certainly guide those who strive and struggle in the cause of the Truth to His path (their destination) because without doubt Allah is with those who lead righteous lives. (29:69)

The Path of the Muslims

For a Muslim, *jihad* is the only path that can lead him to Allah.

> O Muslims! adhere strictly to the laws of Allah. Try to secure a high rank in His eyes. You will be successful in your efforts by striving and struggling hard in His cause. (5:35)

Without *jihad janna* (life of peace and security) is a distant dream, impossible to realise.

> O Muslims! What do you think? You will enter *Jannat* (just by declaring that you believe in Allah. No). You have yet to prove which of you have strived and struggled hard and have endured steadfastly. (3:141)

Jihad exalts one in ranks

> Those who believe in Allah and the life hereafter, and abandon their homes and struggle in the cause of Allah with their possessions and their persons, rank high in the estimation of Allah. These are the ones who will attain success. (9:20)

By *jihad* one becomes a candidate for Allah's *rahma* (means of protection and sources of nourishment).

> Without doubt those who believe in the Divine Order, migrate (leave their homes so as to) strive and struggle in the cause of Allah are the ones who can rightfully expect and receive Allah's *rahma.* [1] (2:218)

By *jihad* one becomes prosperous and pleasantly ingenious.

> But the Messenger and his companions, who believe in Allah, strive and struggle in the cause of Divine Order with their lives and their possessions. All good things of life are for them and they shall prosper. Allah has prepared for them gardens wherein flow streams and where they shall abide; this indeed is a great achievement. (9:88-89)

Life of a Muslim

Ponder over the life of a Muslim. He is born into the world in order to live in accordance with Divine laws and implement them in the world. He does not change according to the system in which he is born. Rather, he tries to change the system according to his ideology. For this change he sacrifices everything that he has, simply because for him his life and wealth are not an end in themselves but are means to achieve a lofty goal. That objective is to implement the Divine Order in the world.

This revolution is the objective of the life of a Muslim. And to achieve this goal he has to strive and struggle hard. This then is *jihad.* The Quran in simple but impressive style narrates this fact. It states that a Muslim is the guardian of his life and wealth and not the owner.

> Allah has purchased of the believers (in the Divine Order) their persons and their goods; for their (in return) is *Jannat* (peace and security): they fight in His cause, and slay and are slain: a promise binding on Him in Truth, through the Torah (Old Testament), the Gospel (New Testament), and the Quran and who is more faithful to his Covenant than Allah? Then rejoice in the bargain, which you have concluded: that is the achievement supreme. (9:111)

---

[1] See *Rahmat* in Glossary.

In this business there is no loss and no setback, only pure gain.

> O you who believe (in the Divine Order) shall I tell you of a business that will save you from a grievous chastisement? If you believe in Allah and His Messenger then strive and struggle hard in the cause of Allah with your wealth and your persons. This bargain is best for you, if you but only knew. (61:10-11)

Upholding the Truth

The Universe has been created in Truth. Therefore, the ideological mission of a Muslim's life is to uphold this Truth so as to establish the Divine system. He is born for this.

> And endeavour in the cause of Allah because it is your right to strive and struggle in His cause. He has chosen you for a glorious life. For you there is no hardship in *Deen* (system of life). The way of life of your father Abraham is also your way of life. He has named you Muslim. This was your name in earlier Scriptures and in this (Quran). This is because the Messenger is witness over your deeds and you are witness over the rest of the mankind. So establish the system of *Salaat* (political order) and *Zakaat* (economic system for the welfare of the entire humanity). Hold fast (the laws of) Allah. He is your Protecting Friend. The blessed Patron and the blessed Helper! (22:78)

This, then, according to the Quran is striving and struggling regularly in the way of Truth and Justice. This is also the blessed philosophy of regular effort and inquiry in which are concealed the secrets of Life.

> O Muslims! Respond to the call of Allah and His Messenger when He calls you so that you may get life. (8:24)

Eternal Life

"A call to life" means to create an atmosphere in which humaneness thrives. Therefore, mere breathing is not life. Similarly, death is not when breathing stops. The Quran states that those who die in this struggle should not be called 'dead'; they are alive. But we do not understand this fact because we think life ends when one stops breathing.

> (During the struggle for the establishment of the Divine Order one should be prepared even to face death.) If one dies in this struggle one should not be considered dead because one has attained eternal life even though it cannot be perceived (by your present level of knowledge). (2:154)

Even to entertain the thought that a striver in the cause of Allah is dead is prohibited.

> Do not ever think that those who have been slain in the cause of Allah are dead. Say, "They are alive with Allah, well-provided with sustenance, rejoicing in what Allah has bestowed upon them. They are glad because of their sacrifice those who have been left behind are free of fear and anxiety." (3:168)

Therefore, according to the Quran, life is motion and action. When there is no movement and action, it is 'death' though physical life may be of any length. Life without dignity is no life. *That* is the secret of the life of an individual or that of a community.

Why Nations rise and fall

Why do nations rise and fall? There are many answers to this question. One principle is common to all of them in all ages. Only the nation which had the enthusiasm to evolve and to move forward and had the passion to strive for its existence ever survived. But the moment its organs of thought and action exhausted, it was wiped out as if they were *lam yakun-shay-am-mazkuuraa* (a thing unremembered). Ordinary people search external reasons and defects for this fall. But external reasons and defects are like ants carrying a dead insect from one place to another. Nations fall because their internal forces become weak and disorderly.

According to the Quran, enthusiasm to evolve and passion to strive is an immutable law. Therefore, it unambiguously states to the community that has been chosen to protect mankind:

> The secret of your existence is in struggling and striving hard. If you will shy foul from this obligation then other communities will take your place and your history will become stories of the past.

> O Muslims! What has happened to you? When you are asked to march forth in the cause of Allah you do not move as if your feet are rooted in the earth. (It seems) you prefer worldly gains to the blessings of the Hereafter although the gains offered by the life of this world are insignificant in comparison to what the life of the hereafter offers. Remember, if you do not march forth Allah will certainly chastise you with a serious chastisement. He will replace you by another people. You can do no harm to Allah since He has control over everything. (9:38-39)

The secret of life lies in fighting and defeating the forces of Evil. Besides, this struggle takes stock of one's strength and thereby one can gauge as to how much talent one has to live and to move forward. This stock-taking will take different forms:

> This struggle will provide you with many opportunities to test your mettle. You may encounter wars and massacres and also be confronted with scarcity of food and loss of life and property or with devastation of fields and orchards. Such ordeals may take place but ultimately those who remain steadfast and do not waver in their commitment to establish Allah's system will be successful. They meet every challenge saying: "We have dedicated ourselves to the establishment of the Divine system and come what may we will continue advancing towards that goal." They are the people who are considered to be eminently deserving of blessings and laudation by their Creator and Sustainer. They will certainly attain their goal. (2:155-157)

It happened to generations gone by and it will happen to us. There is no change in the laws of Allah.

One will not be exempted from this law simply because of claiming to be a Muslim. One's belief in the Divine Order will be tested. In this test one's actions would count not words.

> Do men think that they will be left alone on saying, "We believe," and they will not be tested? (Mere lip profession of Faith is not enough. They will be tried and tested in the real turmoil of life. And remember) We did test (generations) before them so as to tell them who were true and who were false. (29:2-3)

Putting up Lame Excuses

For this test there is no better touchstone than *jihad.* The Quran unambiguously states this fact in the second section of chapter 48, Surah *Al-Fath* (The Victory). Besides, this section unveils various types of prevarications and false excuses by people who hung back from the duty of *jihad.* Though the immediate reference in these verses is in context of the period when the Quran was being revealed, it has generalised connotation that is not confined in time, space and peoples. However, amongst Muslims this sickness of shying away from the duty of *jihad* began taking roots when the vibrant and life-giving message of Allah was replaced by Persian and Greek thoughts. In short, Sufism fatally injured the enthusiasm of Muslims to struggle and to strive.

Sufism

The decline of Muslim power is directly related to the rise of Sufism, for Sufism preached that the biggest *jihad* is purgation of the Self. And this is done by sitting idly in dark and narrow cells of a monastery and repeatedly uttering the name of Allah. This un-Islamic thought gained ground despite clear instructions and exposition in the Quran about the greater *jihad* (*jihad-e-akbar*).

> *Falaa tuti-il-kaafireena wa jaahidhum-bihee jihaadan-ka-beeraa.*
>
> (O Messenger) do not follow those who reject (the Truth), but strive against them with the utmost strenuousness in accordance (with the Quran). (25:52)

Notable is the phrase *falaa tuti-il-kaafireena* in the above verse unambiguously clarifying the meaning of *jihad-e-akbar* – strive and struggle (*jaahidhum-bihee*) in accordance with the laws enshrined in the Quran against the forces that oppose the Divine Order till obedience remains only for the laws of Allah.

Division by the Clergy

The Quran states that the anchorites and the priests hinder men from the way of Allah (9:34). We have seen how Sufis led the Muslims astray. Now let us consider the part played by the priests. They introduced an innovative concept of division of labour in Islam. According to this, war is for the army and the duty of the priests is to legislate in religious affairs and also to issue religious edicts. The Quran nowhere mentions this grouping. The very idea has been borrowed from the *Manu Simriti* of the Hindus. According to the Quran, enjoining good and forbidding evil is the duty of all Muslims and so is war. In Islam, there is no room for a separate class of priests.

5
SLAVERY

What is human history? It is a story of the hunter and the prey written in blood. Every section of this story is both gruesome and pathetic. But the most morbid part is slavery being a disgraceful blot on humanity. What can be worse than considering fellow human beings your chattel and keep them like cattle? Even this comparison does not give the true picture of the conditions of slaves. The owner of cattle does not throw them to the wolves. But slaves have been actors in this drama too. The best loved diversion of the innately barbarous and inhuman Romans was to throw a helpless slave into the cage of a hungry lion and watch them fight for dear life. Special arenas were prepared for this “sport”.

When the last Messenger began his ministry, he saw that slaves were an important part of the society. But, for this flag-bearer of human equality that he was, this ignominy to humanity was intolerable. He declared that it is not legal for a man to consider another man his property. All men are human beings and therefore equal. This is against human honour and dignity that man should be considered a commodity or cattle. Freedom is the birth- right of man. In a human society slavery should come to an end.

Prisoners of War

At that time, the tradition in the world was that the prisoners of war were taken slaves and subsequently their children were considered born slaves. The Quran closed this fountainhead of slavery. It prohibited making slaves of prisoners of war. They would be released either by taking ransom or in good faith.

> Now when you meet in battle your opponents then it is smiting of the necks until you have routed them; then bind fast the bonds; then either give them a free dismissal afterwards or exact a ransom. (47:4)

Slaves of pre-Quranic Times

The prisoners of war till their release remained State guests. After the closure of the fountain the river of slavery would have dried up on its own. But some time was required for this drying up process. The river already had some water and an outlet for it had to be made. At that time slaves were a common feature of almost every Arab household. Slaves worked on their agricultural lands and slave girls did household chores. In this way they had become an integral part of their social and economic life. By freeing them in one stroke would have created complete disorder and chaos in the Arab society of the time. Not only the masters but also the slaves would have found themselves in difficulties. Besides, the Muslims themselves were not in a position to make proper arrangements for all the freed slaves. Therefore, the circumstances demanded that the process of freeing the slaves and the slave girls be carried out in steps and not *en bloc*. Moreover, only in this way they could have adjusted to the demands of a free society. These slaves, as said earlier, already existed in the Arab society. The Quran has called them *maa-malakat aymaanukum* ['those who are in your possession']. All orders of the Quran in the context of slavery are for these slaves only. Once they gained freedom, the very concept of slavery met its doom. For the slaves who existed were slowly but steadily absorbed in the free society and there was no scope for recruiting new ones. The phrase *maa-malakat aymaanukum* is in the past tense. At every place in the Quran only this tense is used for the slaves. This shows that the Quran is referring to only those slaves and slave girls who already existed in the Arab society.

Methods

The Quran employed various methods for the emancipation and betterment of the slaves who already existed (*maa-malakat aymaanukum*) in the Arab society. First of all it encouraged people to free slaves. The Muslims were urged to be kind and considerate to their slaves. They were told that to emancipate a slave was a meritorious act. They could atone for some of their offences by setting a slave free.

> A Muslim would never kill another Muslim except by mistake. If he kills another Muslim by mistake he should set free a believing slave and pay blood money to the family of the deceased. (4:92)

Freeing the slaves was also to atone for frivolous oaths.

kiswatuhum awtah-reeru raqabah.

> (If you have taken an oath not to partake a particular lawful thing, mind it that) Allah holds you accountable only for oaths taken with serious intent and not for frivolous oaths. The atonement for breaking serious oaths is the feeding of ten poor persons with such food as your family eats, or providing clothes to them or setting a slave free. (5:89)

If a person in a fit of anger calls his wife his mother (to declare his intention of not having any sexual relationship with her at all), this was called *zihar*. This practice now became an offence and could be atoned by setting a slave free.

But those who pronounce the word *Zihar* (mother etc. in state of anger) to their wives then wish to go back on the words they uttered, (it is ordained that such a one) should free a slave. (58:3)

Today, it is hard to understand the difficulty the Arabs had to undergo in such atonements; we can hardly imagine how valuable a slave was to them; it immensely affected their social and economic life because slaves had become part and parcel of their society. In such circumstances it was an act of great courage to free a slave. Hence the Quran has compared it with scaling a mountain during which man loses his breath at every step.

> (But even after these facts) man does not gather strength to scale a mountain. And do you know what scaling a mountain means? It is freeing a slave. (90:11-13)

Manumission

If a slave was noticed to possess the potential to contribute positively to the society by being a free person, a deed for his emancipation was written. Besides, he was given economic support to begin a new life.

> And if any of your slaves ask for a deed in writing (for emancipation) then give them such a deed if you know any good in them; besides, give them something yourselves out of the means which Allah has given to you. (24:33)

After this, the Quran said that marriages of the slaves and the slave girls should be solemnised so that they may begin their family lives and thereby become virtuous members of the society.

> Marry those among you who are single, and the eligible ones among your slaves, male or female. (24:32)

It was decreed that not just the slaves but also 'free' citizens should marry the slave girls.

> Whoever amongst you cannot afford to marry a free believing woman may marry a believing slave girl. If you marry a slave girl do not treat her as inferior (because once she accepts Islam and marries you she is at par with others). Allah knows all about your *Eiman* (conviction in the Divine Order and following it. Remember the only consideration for distinction is *Eiman*, otherwise) the one of you is as the other. (4:25)

Good Behaviour

The masters were instructed to behave properly with good manners with your slaves; one's behaviour towards them should be as good as it was towards one's parents and other near relatives.

> And in dealing with your relatives you must strictly adhere to the laws of Allah and no manmade law should be mixed with them. Accordingly you should do well to: a. parents, b. kin-folk, c. orphans, d. others in need, e. neighbors irrespective of whether they are your relatives or not, f. way-farers who stand in need of your help, and g. those in your charge (slaves) or those who work under you. Allah does not like those who are proud and boastful. (4:36)

Sexual Exploitation

The Arabs, during *jaaheliya* (the pre-Islam Age of Ignorance), as per their custom, maintained sexual relations with their slave girls but never gave them the social status of wives. According to the Quran, that was wrong. If a slave girl has not been freed for one reason or another and the master enjoys sex with her, it was his duty to elevate her to the status of a wife. In this way the Quran by one stroke of the pen changed the derogatory position of a slave girl to the high and axiomatic status of a wife. Their illicit relationships were made lawful. And by giving axiomatic status to the strangeness of their relationship the Quran provided them with equality in marital life and their children were also given due social and legal standing at par with others.

> (Who will be successful?) They are those who guard their modesty. (Successful are those who guard themselves against unlawful sex and every kind of sex perversion). But (lawful) sex with wife or slave girl (elevated to the status of wife) is permitted. (23:5-6)

End of Slavery

Thus the Quran brought an end to slavery. The problem of slaves who already existed in the Arab society was solved and the sources of recruiting new slaves were closed forever. Now the question is: why are methods of eradicating slavery still mentioned in the Quran? The answer is simple: if any community, engrossed with the problem of slavery, embraces Islam then the Islamic State has laws to tackle this predicament.

The Re-emergence of Slavery

With the replacement of Islamic political system by monarchy, the Muslim society again adopted the customs and traditions of *jaaheliya* (ignorant or uncivilised people). This un-Islamic way of life was accepted with such enthusiasm that it has become difficult to find an era in which slave girls in thousands were not present in harems of Muslim sultans. One may ask as to why Muslims reverted to the 'Age of Ignorance' when they had with them the Quran with such clear instructions? Well, they have a backdoor called the Tradition literature through which every brigand thought or act can undauntedly emerge. Therefore, Traditions (*Hadith*) were fabricated in favour of exploiting slave girls. And the tragedy is that these inhuman thoughts and shameless slanders have been attributed to the last Messenger whose piety, modesty, integrity and self-control is beyond doubt. In the six True Books of Tradition (*sihaah e sitta*), there exist such absurd Traditions regarding slave girls that embarrass even the most shameless. We do not have the heart to reproduce them here. Nations opposed to Islam have declared that slavery and prostitution are crime but in the sacred city of Mecca slave girls are openly sold. [1]

> Oh, would that I had died before this and had become a thing of naught, forgotten! (19:23)

This is all due to the Tradition (*hadith*) literature because the Quran had put an end to slavery at a time when no nation had the wisdom to think on these lines. Today's Muslims continue to announce proudly from their pulpits and platforms that Islam put an end to slavery. Yet they themselves are the slaves of tradition and religious folklore.

---

[1] (G.A. Parwez's note): In 1963 press reports indicated that the government of Saudi Arabia had banned slavery. If this is correct then it is a welcome sign.

REFERENCES

Collected Works of Mahatma Gandhi (online) (1998-2007) Berlin: GandhiServe Foundation.
<http://www.gandhiserve.org/cwmg/cwmg.html>

Iqbal, M. (1935) *Baal-e-Jibril.*

Briffault, R. (1919) *The Making of Humanity.* London: George Allen & Unwin Ltd.

Dorsey, G. A. (1931) *Civilisation.* London: Hamilton.

Freud, S. (1953) *Civilisation, War and Death.* London: Hogarth Press and the Institute of Psycho-Analysis.

Inge, W. R. (1910) *The Fall of the Idols* London: Putnam.

Gregory, R. (1940) *Religion in Science and Civilisation.* London: Macmillan & Co. Ltd.

Mencken, H. L. (1934) *Treatise on Right and Wrong.* New York: Alfred A. Knopf.

OTHER BOOKS BY THE AUTHOR

EXPOSITION OF THE HOLY QURAN

VOLUMES I & II

G. A. Parwez

It was in 1983 that Ghulam Ahmad Parwez undertook the project of rendering into English his celebrated work titled *Mafhum-ul-Quran*. He only completed the work up to Surah *Al-Kahaf* (no. 18) – just over half of the text, when he passed away in 1985.

This two volume set differs from most English translations of the Quran in that it is not a simple translation at all; rather it is an exposition. It is a serious human effort to convey the pristine concepts of the Holy Quran. As Parwez himself pointed out, however, the original Arabic text of *Wahi* (Revelation) is eternal and human understanding thereof during any given time should not be taken as the last word on the subject.

Readers will also notice with these two volumes that the use of some of the Quranic terms are retained in their Arabic language rather than being translated into English e.g. *Allah, Deen, Nabi, Rasool, Momin, Kafir,* etc. These concepts have special significance in the Quran and it is not possible to translate them succinctly into English. A glossary of these terms is included for those readers who are unfamiliar with them.

ISLAM: A CHALLENGE TO RELIGION

G. A. Parwez

The title of this book appears to be a paradox for it is almost universally accepted that Islam is one of the major religions of the world. So how could a religion challenge the very institution to which it subscribes? The author has indeed made a successful bid to prove this strange aphorism for the first time in the history of Islamic thought and his research deserves careful study. It is thought-provoking; it is revolutionary, opening a whole new horizon of intellectual endeavour. This book contains the essence of a lifelong study of Islam by an insightful and critical thinker.

Having presented the evidence for his claim that Islam is not a religion, Parwez has lucidly explained what Islam really is, and how it offers the most convincing and enduring answers to those eternal questions which philosophers have asked about the meaning and purpose of life. The book is thus a unique attempt at the rediscovery of Islam, scholarly written and exquisitely presented.

* * *

For further details of these and other publications, including ordering information, please contact:

Islamic Dawn Society

76 Park Road

Ilford, Essex IG1 1SF

Email: bazm.london@talktalk.net

www.ingramcontent.com/pod-product-compliance
Ingram Content Group UK Ltd.
Pitfield, Milton Keynes, MK11 3LW, UK
UKHW041923190726
13854UKWH00003B/1418